Digital Television

K.F. Ibrahim
Senior Lecturer College of North West London

Longman

An imprint of **Pearson Education**

Harlow, England · London · New York · Reading, Massachusetts · San Francisco
Toronto · Don Mills, Ontario · Tokyo · Singapore · Hong Kong · Seoul
Taipei · Amsterdam · Munich · Paris · Milan

Pearson Education Limited
Edinburgh Gate
Harlow
Essex CM20 2JE, England
and Associated Companies throughout the world

ISBN 0 582 43138-7

British Library Cataloguing-in-Publication Data

A catalogue record for this book is available from the British Library.

Set by 35 in 10/12pt Times
Printed in Malaysia, KVP

Contents

List of illustrations

List of tables

Preface

Digital video broadcasting using MPEG-2 specifications is quickly becoming the dominant TV technology throughout the world. Here in Britain, the government is considering switching off analogue television broadcasting altogether by the end of the decade. The technology is also employed in many other applications such as DVD and the Internet.

The book provides a detailed explanation of the encoding and broadcasting processes for both satellite and terrestrial transmission (Chapters 3–7). The decoding process for satellite and terrestrial receivers are covered in Chapters 9 and 10. Chapter 11 deals with the latest video techniques of interactive television, including video on demand and personal video recorders (PVRs). Testing satellite and terrestrial set-top boxes and diagnosing faults caused by the STB itself, as well as those caused by the receiving antennas (satellite dishes or terrestrial aerials) are treated in Chapter 12. Fault diagnosis flow charts for satellite and terrestrial receivers are also provided in Chapter 12. Typical power supply circuits are explained in Chapter 12. Introduction to television systems, digital processing techniques and microprocessor systems are covered in Chapters 1, 2 and 8 respectively. For students who are preparing for an examination in the subject, revision questions and answers are provided together with a full glossary of terms.

The book is intended for practicing TV engineers, students as well as enthusiasts. Practical circuits are used throughout. Here, I wish to acknowledge the assistance of PACE Micro technology in providing me with information and making the circuit diagrams available. I am also grateful to PACE for the access to their servicing workshops.

Fawzi Ibrahim
April 2001

To Alex

1 Introduction to television signals

Television signals are generated by the camera at a studio. These analogue signals are then processed for analogue or digital broadcasting. At the television studio, the scene to be broadcast is projected onto a photosensitive plate located inside the TV cameras. The scene is repeatedly scanned by a very fast electron beam, which ensures that consecutive images differ only slightly. At the receiving end, a cathode ray tube (CRT) is used to recreate the picture by an identical process of scanning a coated screen with a moving electron beam. Persistence of vision then gives the impression of a moving picture in the same way as for a cine film. With standard television broadcasting in the UK, 25 pictures are scanned per second.

Scanning

To explore the scene in detail, the brightness of each 'element' of the picture frame is examined line by line (Fig. 1.1). The electron beam sweeps across the scene from left to right, the sweep, and returns back very quickly, the flyback, to begin the next scan-line, and so on. The number of lines scanned may vary depending on the quality of picture definition required. For standard TV broadcasting, the UK uses 625 lines and the USA uses 525 lines. High definition television (HDTV) uses 1250 lines or more. This chapter concentrates on the standard 625 lines.

The waveform that enables the scanning movement of the electron beam is the sawtooth waveform shown in Fig. 1.2. At the end of each picture scan, the electron beam moves back to the top of the scene and the sequence is repeated. With 625 lines

Fig. 1.1 *Line scanning*

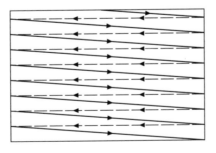

Fig. 1.2 *Scanning sawtooth waveform*

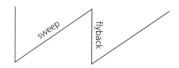

per picture and 25 pictures per second, the scan-line frequency may be calculated as $25 \times 625 = 15\,625$ Hz or 15.625 kHz. The USA uses a rate of 30 pictures per second, giving a line frequency of $30 \times 525 = 15.75$ kHz.

Interlacing

There are two types of scanning, sequential and interlaced. Sequential scanning involves scanning complete 625-line pictures, also called *frames*, at one time, followed by another complete picture scan. Interlaced scanning, on the other hand, involves scanning the odd lines (1, 3, 5, etc.) followed by the even lines (2, 4, 6, etc.). Only half the picture, known as a *field*, is scanned each time, so a complete picture consists of two fields: top (odd) and bottom (even). This results in a field or frame frequency of $2 \times 25 = 50$ Hz. Interlaced scanning avoids the flicker on the television receiver that occurs with sequential scanning.

At the end of each field, the electron beam is deflected rapidly back to the beginning of the next scan. To ensure the same flyback time for both fields, the flyback of the bottom field (lines 2, 4, 6, etc.) is started halfway along the last line of that field (point B in Fig. 1.3) to take the beam to the start of the following top field (lines 1, 3, 5, etc.) which starts halfway along the first scan-line (point C). As can be seen from Fig. 1.3, the beam is made to move through the same vertical distance for both fields. Since the line scan continues to move the beam across the screen, during flyback the beam traces the path shown in Fig. 1.4. With half a line included in each field, the total number of lines must always be odd, hence 625 or 525. In the absence of picture information, scanning produces what is known as a raster.

Fig. 1.3 *The beam moves through the same distance for both fields*

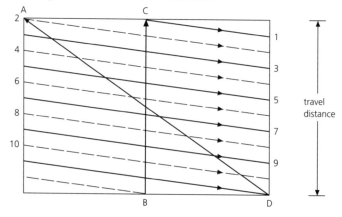

Fig. 1.4 *Flyback path: (a) end of odd field to start of even field, (b) end of even field to start of odd field*

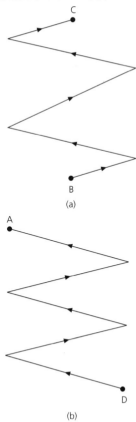

Sync pulses

For faithful reproduction of the picture by the CRT, the scanning at the receiving end must follow the scanning at the transmitting end, line by line and field by field. To ensure this takes place, the TV camera introduces two types of synchronizing pulses (sync pulses): a line sync to indicate the start of a new scan-line and a field sync to indicate the start of a new field.

Composite video waveform

When the sync pulses are added to the picture information, a composite video waveform is produced (Fig. 1.5). The picture information is represented by the waveform between the line sync pulses and thus may acquire any shape, depending on the picture brightness along the scan-line. The waveform shown represents a line that starts at black level then

Fig. 1.5 *Composite video for one scan-line*

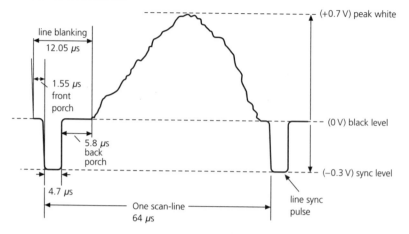

gradually increases in brightness to peak white (maximum brightness) before returning to black level. The total available voltage is divided into two regions:

- *Below black level*: 0–0.3 V reserved for sync pulses (line and field)
- *Above black level*: 0–0.7 V (peak white) used for video or picture information

Before and after every sync pulse the voltage is held at black level for short periods of time, respectively known as the front porch and the back porch. The front porch has a duration of 1.55 μs; it ensures the video information is brought down to the black level before the sync pulse is applied. The back porch has a longer duration of 5.8 μs; it provides time for the flyback to occur before the application of the video information. The front porch, the sync pulse and the back porch are at or below the black level. During this time, a total of 12.05 μs, the video information is completely suppressed; this is known as the line blanking period. For this reason, composite video is frequently known as CVBS (composite video, blanking and sync). The duration of one complete line of composite video may be calculated from the line frequency:

$$\text{line duration} = \frac{1}{\text{line frequency}} = \frac{1}{15.625\,\text{kHz}} = 64\,\mu\text{s}$$

Pixels

The frequency of the video waveform is determined by the change in the brightness of the line as the electron beam scans it. Maximum video frequency is obtained when adjacent active elements, known as *pixels*, are alternately black and white (Fig. 1.6); this represents the maximum definition of a TV image. Along a vertical line there are a maximum of 625 alternating black and white pixels. For equal definition along a horizontal line, the separation between the black and white pixels must be the same as the separation along the vertical line. For a perfectly square television screen, an equal number of pixels would be required in both directions. However, the TV screen has an aspect ratio of

Fig. 1.6 *Maximum video frequency is obtained when adjacent pixels are alternately black and white*

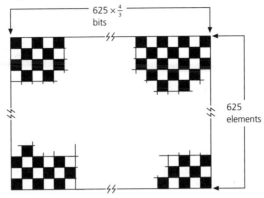

4:3 (digital television uses an aspect ratio of 4:5). The number of horizontal pixels must therefore be increased to $625 \times 4/3 = 833.3$, giving a picture total of

$$625 \times 833.3 = 520\,833 \text{ pixels}$$

Video bandwidth

Fig. 1.7 *Video waveform for alternate black and white elements*

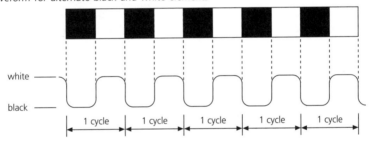

When an electron beam scans a line containing alternate black and white pixels, it produces the video waveform shown in Fig. 1.7, representing the variation in brightness along the scan-line. For any adjacent pair of black and white pixels, one complete cycle is obtained. Hence the ten pixels in Fig. 1.7 produce five complete cycles. It follows that for a complete picture of alternate black and white pixels, the number of cycles is

$$\tfrac{1}{2} \times \text{total number of pixels} = \tfrac{1}{2} \times 520\,833 = 260\,417 \text{ cycles per picture}$$

Since there are 25 complete pictures per second, the number of cycles per second is

$$\text{number of cycles per picture} \times 25 = 260\,417 \times 25$$

$$= 6\,510\,416 \text{ Hz} = 6.5 \text{ MHz}$$

The minimum video frequency is obtained when the electron beam scans pixels of unchanging brightness. This corresponds to unchanging amplitude of the video waveform, a frequency of 0 Hz or DC. The overall bandwidth is therefore 0 Hz to 6.5 MHz. In practice a number of lines are rendered inactive due to blanking of the picture during the flyback period, among other things. This reduces the number of active elements or pixels that have to be scanned, reducing the bandwidth to a more practical 5.5 MHz.

Channel bandwidth

The video information in the form of the CVBS waveform is used to modulate a UHF carrier before transmission. The type of modulation determines the bandwidth of the television channel. Analogue TV broadcasting uses amplitude modulation for the video information. Amplitude modulation produces two sets of sidebands, one on either side of the carrier, thus doubling the bandwidth requirement. However, since each sideband contains all the video information, it is possible to suppress one sideband completely, employing what is known as a single-sideband (SSB) transmission. However, pure single-sideband transmission demands a more complicated synchronous detector at the receiving end, making the receiver more expensive. The simple and cheap diode detector may be used, but it introduces quadrature distortion caused mainly by the lower end of the video frequency spectrum. To avoid this, *vestigial sideband transmission* is employed in which double-sideband transmission is used for the low video frequencies and single-sideband transmission for higher video frequencies. Figure 1.8 shows the frequency response of analogue TV transmission in the UK in which part of the lower sideband, up to 1.25 MHz, is transmitted with the upper sideband.

As well as the composite video, it is also necessary to transmit sound signals. Sound is frequency modulated on a separate carrier with a bandwidth of 100 kHz. The sound

Fig. 1.8 *Frequency response for analogue TV transmission: monochrome*

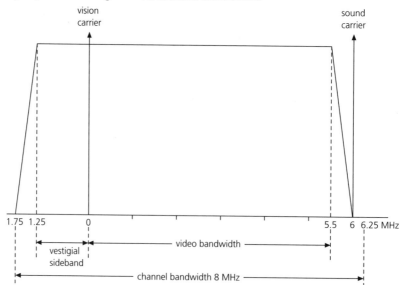

Fig. 1.9 *Frequency response for analogue TV transmission: colour*

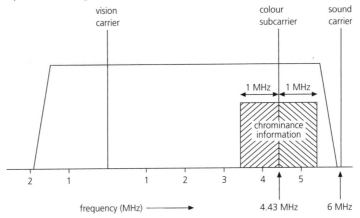

carrier is chosen to be 6 MHz away from the vision carrier, so it falls just outside the highest transmitted video frequency.

Figure 1.8 shows how the frequency response remains constant over the range of video frequencies up to 5.5 MHz on the upper sideband and up to 1.25 MHz on the lower sideband. Above 5.5 MHz a sharp but gradual attenuation takes place to ensure that no video information remains above 6 MHz; this prevents any overlap with the sound information. An additional 0.25 MHz is needed to accommodate the sound bandwidth and to provide a buffer space for the adjacent channel. Similar attenuation is necessary for frequencies extending beyond 1.25 MHz on the lower sideband to ensure that no information extends beyond 1.75 MHz, thus preventing any overlap with adjacent channels. An 8 MHz (1.75 + 6.25) bandwidth must therefore be allocated for each analogue TV channel.

Principles of colour TV transmission

Colour transmission is based on two facts. The first is that all colours may be produced by the addition of appropriate quantities of the three *primary colours*: red (*R*), green (*G*) and blue (*B*). For example,

$$\text{yellow} = R + G$$
$$\text{magenta} = R + B$$
$$\text{cyan} = B + G$$
$$\text{white} = R + G + B$$

Yellow, magenta and cyan are known as *complementary colours*, complementary to blue, green and red respectively.

The second fact is that the human eye reacts predominantly to the luminance (black and white) component of a colour picture, much more than to its chrominance (colour) component.

Colour TV transmission involves the simultaneous transmission of the luminance and chrominance components of a colour picture, with luminance predominant over chrominance. In analogue TV broadcasting, the luminance signal Y representing the luminance component is transmitted directly in the same way as a monochrome transmission. This provides the necessary compatibility between the two systems. As for the chrominance component, it is first 'purified' by removing the luminance component from each primary colour, resulting in what is known as colour difference signals:

$$R - Y \qquad G - Y \qquad B - Y$$

Since the luminance signal $Y = R + G + B$, only two colour difference signals need to be transmitted, namely $R - Y$ and $B - Y$. The third colour difference, $G - Y$, may be recovered at the receiver from the three transmitted components: Y, $R - Y$ and $B - Y$. In analogue TV broadcasting, the two colour difference signals $R - Y$ and $B - Y$ are known as U and V respectively. In digital television, they are referred to as C_R and C_B.

The additional chrominance information $R - Y$ and $B - Y$ is added to the monochrome information by the introduction of a subcarrier of 4.43 MHz. Quadrature amplitude modulation (QAM) is used in which the two colour difference signals are used to modulate one of two quadrature (right angles) 4.43 MHz subcarriers. The bandwidth of the chrominance information is limited to 1 MHz on each side of the subcarrier (Fig. 1.9). The relatively narrow bandwidth allocated to the chrominance signal is quite sufficient for faithful reproduction of a colour image at the receiving end. This is because the human eye perceives high video frequencies in black and white only. The colour subcarrier is chosen to be a multiple of half the line frequency to ensure that its side frequencies fall between the side frequencies produced by the monochrome signal, a process known as frequency interleaving. Finally, a sample (about 10 cycles) of the subcarrier, known as *colour burst*, is transmitted for use as a reference at the receiving end. The colour burst is mounted on the back porch of the line sync.

The PAL colour system

There are three main systems of analogue colour encoding: NTSC, PAL and SECAM. All three systems split the colour picture into luminance and chrominance; all three use colour difference signals to transmit the chrominance information. The difference between the three systems lies in the way the subcarrier is modulated by the colour difference signals. SECAM (used in France) transmits the colour difference signals on alternate lines. The other two systems, NTSC (used in the USA) and PAL (used in the UK), transmit both chrominance components simultaneously using quadrature amplitude modulation. However, it is found that errors in hue may occur as a result of phase errors (delay or advance) of the chrominance phasor. Such errors are caused either by the receiver itself or by the way the signal is propagated. They are almost completely corrected by PAL.

In the PAL (phase alternate line) system, the V signal is reversed on successive lines: V on one line is followed by $-V$ on the next, and so on. The first line is called the NTSC line and the second is called a PAL line. Phasor errors are thus reversed from one line to the next. At the receiving end, a process of averaging takes place either by the human eye (PAL-S) or by employing a delay line to allow for consecutive lines (NTSC and PAL) to be added to each other, thus cancelling any phase errors. This latter technique is known as PAL-D.

2 Introduction to digital processing

Binary and hex

Unlike analogue signals, which are continuous and may theoretically take an infinite number of instantaneous values, a digital signal uses the binary system with two discrete values: logic 0 and logic 1. A single binary digit, known as a *bit*, can thus have one of two values or states: a 0 or low and a 1 or high. The amount of information that can be exchanged using one bit only is very limited (on or off, yes or no, 0 or 1). More information may be conveyed by grouping a number of bits together to form what is known as a word. A word using 2 bits, a 2-bit word, may be used to represent four different combinations ($2^2 = 4$) as shown in Table 2.1.

A 3-bit word gives a further doubling to $2^3 = 8$ different combinations (Table 2.2), and so on. A 4-bit word, known as a *nibble*, provides $2^4 = 16$ different combinations and an 8-bit word, known as a *byte*, provides $2^8 = 256$ different combinations.

Binary numbers

In the same way as denary (decimal) columns represent increasing powers of 10, binary columns represent increasing powers of 2; the rightmost bit is known as the *least significant bit (LSB)* and has a value of $2^0 = 1$. The next column has a value of $2^1 = 2$, the next $2^2 = 4$, and so on (Table 2.3). In any binary number, the leftmost bit is known as the *most significant bit (MSB)*. Each logic level is represented by a voltage level. For TTL (transistor–transistor logic) technology, a logic high (logic 1) is represented by a high voltage between 2.8 and 5 V and a logic low (logic 0) is represented by a low voltage between 0 and 0.4 V (Fig. 2.1).

Table 2.1 Combinations with two bits

Bit 1	Bit 0
0	0
0	1
1	0
1	1

Table 2.2 Combinations with three bits

Bit 2	Bit 1	Bit 0
0	0	0
0	0	1
0	1	0
0	1	1
1	0	0
1	0	1
1	1	0
1	1	1

Table 2.3 Binary columns

2^4	2^3	2^2	2^1	2^0	
(16)	(8)	(4)	(2)	(1)	
1	0	0	1	1	$= 1 \times 16 + 0 \times 8 + 0 \times 4 + 1 \times 2 + 1 \times 1 = 16 + 2 + 1 = 19$
0	1	1	0	1	$= 0 \times 16 + 1 \times 8 + 1 \times 4 + 0 \times 2 + 1 \times 1 = 8 + 4 + 1 = 13$

Fig. 2.1 *Logic levels for TTL*

Hexadecimal

To avoid long strings of binary digits, hexadecimal notation is used. Hexadecimal numbers have a base of 16, hence there are 16 distinct symbols:

0, 1, 2, 3, 4, 5, 6, 7, 8, 9, A, B, C, D, E, F

with A, B, C, D, E, F representing denary numbers 10, 11, 12, 13, 14 and 15 respectively. A single hexadecimal digit (Table 2.4) may therefore represent each 4-bit denary number. An 8-bit binary number is represented by a two-digit hexadecimal number and a 12-bit binary number by a three-digit hexadecimal number (Fig. 2.2). A common way of distinguishing binary and hexadecimal numbers is to terminate binary numbers with B and hexadecimal numbers with H. For instance, binary 0010 is written 0010B and hexadecimal 2F is written 2FH.

Table 2.4 Converting hexadecimal to binary	
Hexadecimal	Binary
0	0000
1	0001
2	0010
3	0011
4	0100
5	0101
6	0110
7	0111
8	1000
9	1001
A	1010
B	1011
C	1100
D	1101
E	1110
F	1111

Fig. 2.2 *Binary–hex conversion*

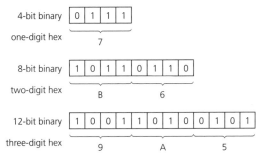

Logic gates

A logic gate is a device whose output depends on the instantaneous combination of its inputs. For instance, an AND gate produces a logic 1 (high) output if and only if all its inputs are high. The different types of gates, their symbols and truth tables are listed in Tables 2.5 and 2.6.

Serial and parallel communication

A digital package of information consists of a number of bits grouped together to form a word which is the basic unit of information, e.g. an 8-bit word or a 16-bit word. A word can only make sense when all the bits have been received. In serial transmission

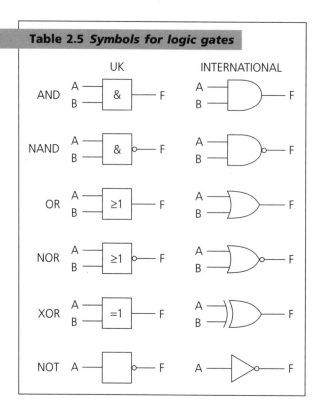

Table 2.5 Symbols for logic gates

	UK	INTERNATIONAL
AND	A B & F	A B F
NAND	A B & F	A B F
OR	A B ≥1 F	A B F
NOR	A B ≥1 F	A B F
XOR	A B =1 F	A B F
NOT	A F	A F

Table 2.6 Truth tables for logic gates

Inputs		Output function				
A	B	AND	NAND	OR	NOR	XOR
0	0	0	1	0	1	0
0	1	0	1	1	0	1
1	0	0	1	1	0	1
1	1	1	0	1	0	0

the bits are sent one at a time along a single line (Fig. 2.3); in parallel transmission the bits are transmitted simultaneously (Fig. 2.4).

Shift registers

A shift register is a temporary store of data, which may then be sent out in a serial or parallel form. Figure 2.5 shows an 8-bit shift register where serial data is clocked into the register, bit by bit. When the register is full, the data stored in the register may then be clocked out serially, bit by bit. This type of shift register is called a *serial-in serial-out*

Fig. 2.3 *Serial transmission*

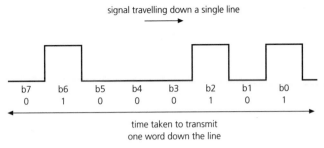

signal travelling down a single line

b7	b6	b5	b4	b3	b2	b1	b0
0	1	0	0	0	1	0	1

time taken to transmit
one word down the line

Fig. 2.4 *Parallel transmission*

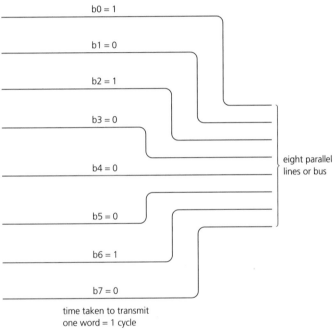

b0 = 1

b1 = 0

b2 = 1

b3 = 0

b4 = 0

b5 = 0

b6 = 1

b7 = 0

eight parallel
lines or bus

time taken to transmit
one word = 1 cycle

Fig. 2.5 *SISO shift register*

serial data → | b0 | b1 | b2 | b3 | b4 | b5 | b6 | b7 | → serial data out

clock →

(SISO) shift register. Three other arrangements are possible: *serial-in parallel-out (SIPO)*, *parallel-in serial-out (PISO)* and *parallel-in parallel-out (PIPO)*.

Digital codes

The conversion of a quality or a number into a digital format may be carried out using one of several codes. In the natural binary code in Table 2.8 the columns represent

Table 2.7 *Binary-coded decimal*

Denary number	BCD
00	0000 0000
01	0000 0001
02	0000 0010
03	0000 0011
04	0000 0100
05	0000 0101
06	0000 0110
07	0000 0111
08	0000 1000
09	0000 1001
10	0001 0000
11	0001 0001
:	: :
57	0101 0111
:	: :
83	1000 0011
:	: :
99	1001 1001

progressively increasing powers of 2, which gives a count of 0 to 15. Such a count is not very appropriate for denary applications. A more appropriate coding technique is *binary-coded decimal (BCD)*, which converts each denary digit into a 4-bit binary number. A two-digit BCD number will thus result in two groups of 4-bit binary numbers (8 bits in total) as illustrated in Table 2.7.

Another popular coding technique is the Gray code; this ensures that only one binary bit changes state as the denary number is progressively incremented (Table 2.8). The Gray code avoids the problems of spurious transitional codes associated with the BCD technique.

Multiplexing

Communication invariably involves transmitting several programmes via the same communication media, such as cable, satellite or terrestrial links. This may be achieved in two ways: broadband using frequency division multiplexing (FDM) and baseband using time division multiplexing (TDM). Frequency division techniques involve dividing the available bandwidth into several channels; each channel is then allocated to a single programme. The programmes are thus transmitted simultaneously. But in time division multiplexing the programmes are transmitted sequentially. Each programme is allocated

Table 2.8 *Gray coding*		
Denary	Binary code	Gray code
0	0000	0000
1	0001	0001
2	0010	0011
3	0011	0010
4	0100	0110
5	0101	0111
6	0110	0101
7	0111	0100
8	1000	1100
9	1001	1101
10	1010	1111
11	1011	1110
12	1100	1010
13	1101	1011
14	1110	1001
15	1111	1000

Fig. 2.6 *Multiplexing*

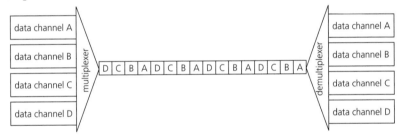

a time slot during which the whole of the bandwidth of the medium is made available to it. At the receiving end, the transmitted data is demultiplexed to obtain the required programme (Fig. 2.6). Time division multiplexing is most efficient if all programmes carry the same amount of data. If they do not, i.e. if the traffic level is uneven, some time slots will be underutilized while other time slots may not be able to handle the data stream.

Statistical multiplexing

To avoid this, a technique called statistical TDM is used in which the allocation of time slots is based on the amount of traffic each programme generates. Time slots are allocated according to need (Fig. 2.7). Programmes that generate heavy traffic are allocated more time slots while those with lighter traffic are allocated fewer time slots.

Fig. 2.7 *Statistical multiplexing*

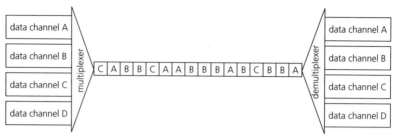

Memory chips

Basic organization

Memory chips are data storage devices where information in the form of software programs or text may be saved. A memory chip contains a number of locations. Each location stores one or more bits of data, known as its *bit width*, and each location is identified by a unique address. Figure 2.8 shows the basic organization of a memory chip. Each location stores 8 bits of data, known as a byte, and each location is given a unique binary address. A 3-bit address (A0, A1 and A2) provides a maximum of $2^3 = 8$ memory locations. A 10-bit address (A0 to A9) has $2^{10} = 1024$ or 1 K memory locations (Fig. 2.8). The address lines are grouped together to form an address bus. By placing an address

Fig. 2.8 *Basic organization of a memory chip*

	ADDRESS		DATA	
	A9 ◄—— Binary —— A0	Hex	8 bits 1 byte D7 ◄—————— D0	
Address bits	0 0 0 0 0 0 0 0 0 0	000	x x x x x x x x	
	0 0 0 0 0 0 0 0 0 1	001	x x x x x x x x	Data bits
A9 ——►	0 0 0 0 1 1 1 1 1 1	03F	x x x x x x x x	
A8 ——►	0 0 0 0 0 0 0 1 0 0	040	x x x x x x x x	——► D7
A7 ——►				——► D6
A6 ——►				——► D5
A5 ——►	0 0 1 0 1 0 1 1 1 1	0AF	x x x x x x x x	——► D4
A4 ——►	0 0 1 0 1 1 0 0 0 0	0B0	x x x x x x x x	——► D3
A3 ——►				——► D2
A2 ——►	0 0 1 0 1 1 0 1 0 1	0B5	x x x x x x x x	——► D1
A1 ——►				——► D0
A0 ——►				
	0 0 1 1 1 1 1 1 1 1	0FF	x x x x x x x x	
	0 1 0 0 0 0 0 0 0 0	100	x x x x x x x x	
	1 1 1 1 1 1 1 1 1 0	FFE	x x x x x x x x	
	1 1 1 1 1 1 1 1 1 1	FFF	x x x x x x x x	

on the address bus, any one of the 1024 locations may be selected. For instance, if A9, A8, ..., A1, A0 are set to logic levels 0, 0, 1, 0, 1, 1, 0, 1, 0, 1, then the location with address 0010110101 in binary (0B5 in hexadecimal) is selected. For simplicity, addresses are normally stated in hexadecimal. Once a memory location is chosen, pins D0 to D7 on the chip provide access to the eight memory cells in that location. Data is also normally stated in hexadecimal. Memory chips have two main properties: storage capacity, or size, and access time, or speed.

Storage capacity

The storage capacity of a memory chip is the number of locations multiplied by the width of the data bus. For example, a chip with 512 locations and a 2-bit data width has a memory size of

$$512 \times 2 = 1024 \text{ bits}$$

Since the standard unit of data is a byte (8 bits), storage capacity is normally given as

$$1024/8 = 128 \text{ bytes}$$

The number of locations is determined by the number of address pins that are provided. For example, a chip with 10 address lines has $2^{10} = 1024$ or 1 K locations. Given an 8-bit data width, a 10-bit address chip has a memory size of

$$2^{10} \times 8 = 1024 \times 8 = 1 \text{ K} \times 1 \text{ byte} = 1 \text{ kilobyte or } 1 \text{ KB}$$

A single chip is usually insufficient to provide the memory requirements of a computer. A number of chips are therefore connected in parallel to form what is known as a memory bank.

Access time

Access time measures how quickly a location in the memory chip may be made available to the data bus. It is defined as the time interval between the instant that an address is sent to the memory chip and the instant that the data stored into the location appears on the data bus. Access time is given in nanoseconds (ns) and varies from 5 ns to the relatively slow 200 ns.

Types of memory (Table 2.9)

Random access memory

Random access memory (RAM) is a memory chip which the user may read from or write into, hence it is also known as read/write memory. RAM chips are known as volatile because their contents are lost when power is switched off. Locations may be accessed at random by placing the address of the selected location onto the address lines. The pin-out requirements of a RAM chip are shown in Fig. 2.9. Apart from the address lines and the data bits, there are three control lines, all of them active low: write enable (WE) goes low when the CPU wishes to write new data into the selected location; output enable

Table 2.9 *Memory device comparison*

	DRAM	SRAM	ROM	EPROM	EEPROM	Flash
Capacity	Mbytes	kbytes	kbytes	kbytes	kbytes	kbytes
Speed (ns)	60–120	25–40	200	400	400	100
Lifespan	long	long	long	short	short	short

Fig. 2.9 *RAM chip standard pin-out*

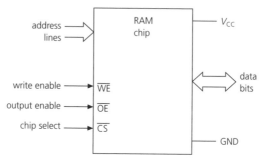

(OE) goes low when the processor wishes to read the contents of the location; and chip select (CS) is driven low when the selected location falls within the range address assigned for the chip.

There are two major categories of RAM: dynamic RAM (*DRAM*) and static RAM (*SRAM*). Dynamic RAMs store information in the form of a charge on a capacitor. However, due to leakage, the charge is lost and has to be restored at frequent intervals of between 2 and 4 ms, a process known as *refreshing* the cells. Dynamic RAMs have the advantage of higher component density (hence small size) and very low power consumption. Static RAMs employ flip-flops (electronic switching devices) as the basic cell and hence require no refreshing. They will hold data as long as DC power continues to be applied to the device. SRAMs are very fast with an access time of 5 ns or less compared with 60 ns for DRAMs. However, they are more expensive and larger in size than the dynamic type, which inhibits their use as the main memory store of a computer system.

Because of their low cost and high component density, DRAM devices and the faster synchronous DRAM (SDRAM) are used to provide most computer memory of few megabytes. The number of address pins required to accommodate this size of memory becomes physically inhibitive for manufacturing purposes. To overcome this problem, address multiplexing is employed. The multiplexer receives the full 20-bit address from the address bus, which is then fed to the memory chip in two stages. First A0–A9 are fed to the address pins on the IC then A10–A19 are fed to the same IC pins. Two special control signals, column address strobe (*CAS*) and row address strobe (*RAS*), are provided to route the two halves to two internal latches. The full address is then held within the IC long enough to access the data in the selected location. A typical pin-out is shown in Fig. 2.10.

Fig. 2.10 *Dynamic RAM: typical pin-out*

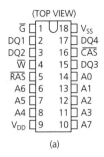

(TOP VIEW)

$\overline{G}$	1	18	V_{SS}
DQ1	2	17	DQ4
DQ2	3	16	$\overline{CAS}$
$\overline{W}$	4	15	DQ3
$\overline{RAS}$	5	14	A0
A6	6	13	A1
A5	7	12	A2
A4	8	11	A3
V_{DD}	9	10	A7

(a)

PIN NOMENCLATURE	
A0–A7	Address inputs
$\overline{CAS}$	Column address strobe
DQ1–DQ4	Data in/data out
$\overline{G}$	Output enable
$\overline{RAS}$	Row address strobe
V_{DD}	+5 V supply
V_{SS}	Ground
$\overline{W}$	Write enable

(b)

Backup battery

One method of preserving the stored data in a normal RAM is to employ backup batteries to maintain the DC supply voltage to the chip when the mains supply is removed.

Read-only memory

Read-only memories (ROMs) are non-volatile in that they retain their data irrespective of the power supply. ROM devices are slow compared with RAM; they have a typical access time in excess of 200 ns. This makes them unsuitable for applications that require fast memory access such as video applications. There are several types of ROM device.

Mask ROM is a non-volatile memory used for storing data permanently. The stored data can only be read by the user and no new data can be written into the device. ROM is programmed by the manufacturer in accordance with predetermined specifications. Once entered, the data cannot be altered.

Programmable read-only memories (*PROMs*) fulfil the same basic function as ROM devices except that they may be programmed by the user, known as blowing the chip. Once programmed, PROMs cannot be altered.

Erasable programmable read-only memories (*EPROMs*) overcome this by allowing the user to delete or erase the stored data and thus change the program. The stored program in an EPROM may be erased by exposing the memory cells to ultraviolet light through a window on the IC package. It takes 20–30 minutes to return the IC to a 'blank state' ready to be reprogrammed.

Electrically erasable programmable read-only memories (*EEPROMs*) can be programmed and erased while still connected to the circuit, by the application of suitable electrical signals. Furthermore, individual locations may be erased and programmed without interfering with the rest of the data pattern. As a result of overwriting, EEPROM has a comparatively short lifespan.

Flash RAM

Flash RAM is an advance on EEPROM. All flash RAM locations may be erased and reprogrammed, except this time using normal voltages that are available in the receiver. However, flash RAM continues to suffer from a short lifespan and a long access time of 60–150 ns.

Analogue-to-digital conversion

In most applications the initial information such as video or audio is in the form of an analogue signal, which must be converted into a digital format before digital processing can take place. Analogue-to-digital conversion consists of two distinct stages: sampling and quantizing (Fig. 2.11). Sampling is the process of assessing the value of the analogue signal at regular intervals. The samples are then rounded to the nearest predetermined level, a process known as quantization. The amplitude of each sample may be represented by a binary code, a process known as pulse code modulation (PCM). The number of bits used to identifiy each pulse is determined by the number of quantized levels. For instance, 8 different levels require 3 bits, 64 levels require 6 bits, and so on. Conversely, the number of available quantized levels is determined by the bit width of the converter. A 3-bit converter provides $3^2 = 8$ levels, an 8-bit converter provides $2^8 = 256$ levels, and so on. Table 2.10 lists all possible outputs of a 3-bit ADC with a quantum of 0.25 V. At the receiving end, the samples are reproduced at their quantified levels and their peaks are joined to reconstruct the original analogue signal (Fig. 2.12).

Fig. 2.11 *Analogue-to-digital conversion*

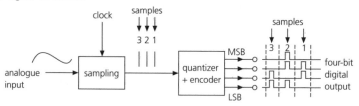

Fig. 2.12 *Waveform reconstruction*

Sampling rates

The Shannon sampling theory states that sampling an analogue signal does not remove any information provided that the sampling rate is no less than twice the highest analogue frequency. This sampling rate is known as the *Nyquist rate*, which ensures that the reconstructed waveform at the receiving end contains all the information of the original analogue signal. If the sampling rate is lower than the Nyquist rate, an overlap occurs between the sidebands produced by the sampling process. This creates an effect known as *aliasing*, which makes it impossible to recover the original signal without distortion. However, recovering signals that have been sampled at the Nyquist rate requires an ideal filter with a very sharp cut-off, a situation that must be avoided. In practice, a sampling rate which is slightly higher than the Nyquist rate (about 10% higher) is used to provide enough separation between the sidebands, allowing practical filters to be used.

Quantizing error

With the input being analogue, sample values will invariably fall between the pre-determined discrete quantized levels (Table 2.10). Hence there is always an element of uncertainty in terms of the actual value of the least significant bit (LSB). This ambiguity gives rise to what is known as the *quantizing error*, an error that is inherent in any digital coding of analogue values. The effect of this type of noise is that some data bits are received incorrectly, distorting the reconstructed waveform.

Quantized error has a constant quantity equal to one-half the quantum. The effect of quantized noise is therefore more noticeable when the analogue signal is at a low level, resulting in poor signal-to-noise ratio (SNR). Assuming a quantum level of 250 mV, the quantized error will be

$$\tfrac{1}{2} \times \text{quantum} = \tfrac{1}{2} \times 250 = 125 \text{ mV}$$

If the analogue signal is strong, say 1.5 V, then

$$\text{SNR} = 1.5/0.125 = 12 \quad \text{or} \quad 20 \log 12 = 21.6 \text{ dB}$$

Table 2.10 *Quantized levels*

| Level | Sample voltage (V) | Binary code | | |
		MSB		LSB
0	0	0	0	0
1	0.25	0	0	1
2	0.50	0	1	0
3	0.75	0	1	1
4	1.00	1	0	0
5	1.25	1	0	1
6	1.50	1	1	0
7	1.75	1	1	1

If the analogue signal is weak, say 0.25 V, then

$$\text{SNR} = 0.25/0.125 = 2 \quad \text{or} \quad 20 \log 2 = 6 \text{ dB}$$

Bit rate

The bit rate is defined as the number of bits produced per second by the encoder. Given a sampling frequency of f_s and an n-bit quantizer, the bit rate generated is given by

bit rate $= n \times f_s$ bits per second

An 8-bit analogue-to-digital converter (ADC) with a sampling frequency of 10 MHz generates a bit rate of 8×10 MHz $= 80$ Mbit/s.

Fig. 2.13 *Maximum frequency occurs when adjacent bits alternate between 0 and 1*

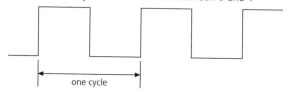

one cycle

Bandwidth requirements

The bandwidth requirement of a communication channel is the maximum frequency that may be produced by the bitstream. This maximum frequency is determined by the bit rate generated by the quantizing encoder. The maximum rate of change of a bitstream, i.e. the maximum frequency, is obtained when adjacent bits alternate between 0 and 1 (Fig. 2.13). One complete cycle of the waveform, periodic time T, contains 2 bits. It follows therefore that the frequency of the waveform is half the bit rate, giving a bandwidth of $\frac{1}{2}$ bit rate. In other words, a channel with bandwidth B has a capacity of $2B$ pulses per second. This is the theoretical value. In practice this capacity is reduced somewhat to kB where k is between 1 and 2, depending, among other things, on the shape and width of the pulses.

Channel capacity

Up to 1948, when Shannon published *The Mathematical Theory of Communication*, it was assumed that because of the presence of random noise in a channel, error-free transmission could only be achieved if the bit rate approached zero. However, Shannon proved that random noise does not, by itself, set any limit on the accuracy of the transmission. Instead, noise sets a limit on the rate of information (the bit rate) that can be achieved in a channel in which the probability of error is very small or approaching zero, what is known as a virtually error-free communication system. Shannon proved that the limitation imposed on channel capacity C is determined by the available bandwidth B and the signal-to-noise ratio SNR:

$$C = B \log_2(1 + \text{SNR}) \text{ bits per second}$$

If there were no noise on the channel, there would never be any uncertainty in the received pulses and thus capacity C would be infinite. Communications would cease to be a problem. However, for a given SNR, the bandwidth will determine the bit rate that can be achieved for an error-free environment. Conversely, given a channel bandwidth, the SNR will determine the maximum bit rate that may be achieved. It follows that bandwidth and SNR are interchangeable and may be traded against each other in the design of any communication system. The relationship between bandwidth and SNR is logarithmic, so a relatively small increase in bandwidth may be traded for a large improvement in SNR and consequently a large reduction in transmitted signal power.

Non-linear quantization

Although the quantization error cannot be wholly avoided, it can be minimized by improving the resolution of the converter through increasing its bit width and thus reducing the quantized level, the quantization error and the quantization noise. However, this still leaves weak signals with a comparatively poor SNR. To overcome this, non-linear quantizing may be used, in which the quantum level for weak signals is decreased (i.e. more bits are utilized to represent them) compared with the quantum level for strong signals. This type of non-linear quantization, known as *companding*, tends to equalize the SNR over the range of sample amplitudes generated by the analogue signal. At the receiving end, a complementary non-linear digital-to-analogue converter (DAC) is employed to reproduce the original analogue signal. Another technique which accomplishes a similar result is to use an analogue voltage compressor to precede the linear encoder at the transmitting end, a process known as *pre-emphasis*. The compressed analogue voltage gives prominence to weaker signals. At the receiving end, the process is reversed using a voltage expander.

In many applications, such as digital audio or video processing, linear quantization produces a bit rate which may be higher than can be accommodated by the available bandwidth. To rectify this, a controlled quantizer is used which can vary the resolution of the encoder to ensure a constant bit rate at its output. This is carried out dynamically as the input data stream varies in quantity and speed.

Error control techniques

In all types of communication system, errors may be minimized but they cannot be avoided completely, hence the need for error correction techniques. If an error is detected at the receiving end, it can be corrected in two different ways: the recipient can request the original transmitter for a repeat of the transmission, or the recipient can attempt to correct the errors without any further information from the transmitter. Whenever it is a realistic option, communication systems tend to go for retransmission. But if the distances are large, perhaps to contact a space probe, or if real-time signals are involved, such as in audio and video broadcasting, then retransmission is not an option. These cases require error correction techniques.

Error correction makes use of redundancy in messages. In ordinary English, the *u* following a *q* is quite unnecessary and 'at this moment in time' can be shortened to 'at this moment' or even 'now'. Redundant letters or words play a very important role in

Fig. 2.14 *Parity*

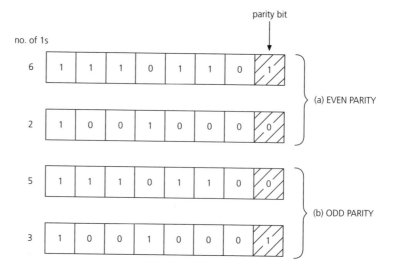

communication. They allow the recipient to make sense of distorted information. This is how we can make sense of badly spelled postcards, a corrupted fax, a badly tuned receiver, and so on.

In digital communications, redundancy means unnecessary data that occupies precious bandwidth. For this reason, compression techniques are used to ensure that only necessary data is transmitted; in video and audio broadcasting, raw data is compressed by a hundred times or more to reduce the bandwidth requirements. This leaves no room for error correction. For this reason, controlled redundancy bits are added to enable messages corrupted in transmission to be corrected at the receiving end.

The most basic technique, *parity*, provides rudimentary error detection. It involves a single parity bit at the end of a digital word to indicate whether the number of 1s is even or odd (Fig. 2.14). There are two types of parity checking. Even parity (Fig. 2.14a) is when the complete coded data, including the parity bit, contains an even number of 1s. Odd parity (Fig. 2.14b) is when the complete coded data contains an odd number of 1s. At the receiving end, the number of 1s is counted and checked against the parity bit; a difference indicates an error. This simple parity check can only detect an error occurring in a single bit. An error affecting two bits will go undetected. Furthermore, there is no provision for determining which bit is actually faulty. For this reason, more sophisticated techniques are normally used with high levels of redundancy. One such technique is forward error correction (FEC) employed in digital television broadcasting.

Forward error correction

The introduction of redundancy bits to a package of data increases the data length and with it the number of possible combinations. Consider a 6-bit package consisting of 4 bits of useful data and 2 redundancy bits. The 4 bits of useful data contain $2^4 = 16$ different valid messages. At the receiving end, however, a set of $2^6 = 64$ different messages may

Table 2.11 *Invalid code words*

Nearest to 010	Nearest to 101
011	001
110	100
000	111

be received, of which only a subset contains the 16 valid messages. This subset is called a *code* and the valid messages are called *code words* or *code vectors* (vectors for short). When a message is received that does not correspond to any of the valid code words, the receiver finds a valid code word 'nearest' to the received message, on the assumption that the nearest is the most likely correct message. This technique is known as *forward error correction (FEC)*. As an example, consider a 1-bit word extended to a 3-bit word by the addition of two redundant bits. The 1-bit word has two valid messages, 1 and 0, which are now being represented by 3-bit codes, say 010 and 101. These are the only valid code words out of a total of $2^3 = 8$. It follows that if any of the other remaining six code words are received – 000, 001, 011, 100, 110 and 111 – an error has occurred during transmission, an error which must be corrected. The invalid code words can be divided into those which are nearest to 010, i.e. those that differ from 010 by one digit only, and those nearest to 101, i.e. those that differ from 101 by one digit only (Table 2.11).

Suppose the invalid code word 011 is received; it can be corrected because it is most likely intended to be 010 with the last digit corrupted. It could have been 101 with the first two bits corrupted to make 011, but that is less likely as the probability of one bit error in three is significantly greater than the probability of two bit errors in three. Real codes contain very long strings of binary bits with thousands of valid code words, which makes it impractical to use this simple comparison method. For this reason, carefully designed codes are used to produce code words which are well structured into sets and subsets. The process of correction is then carried out by sophisticated mathematics. There are two coding techniques: *block coding* and *convolutional coding*.

In block codes, such as Hamming or Reed–Solomon codes, a block of k data digits is encoded by a code generator (Fig. 2.15) into a code word of n digits where n is larger than k. The number of redundancy bits is therefore $(n - k)$. The ratio k/n represents the efficiency of the code and is normally known as the *code rate*. In convolutional codes, the coded sequence from the encoder depends not only on the sequence of the incoming block of k bits, but also on the sequence of data bits that preceded it. Unlike block codes, the code word of a convolutional code is not unique to the incoming k bits, but depends on earlier data as well. For convolutional codes, k and n are usually small, giving small code rates such as 1/2, 3/4 and 7/8.

Fig. 2.15 *Code generator*

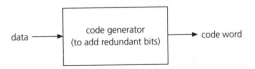

Fig. 2.16 *Bit interleaving*

Original bit sequence	0	1	2	3	4	5	6	7
After interleaving	2	5	7	1	4	6	0	3
Lost bits due to interference				×	×	×		
Damaged bit sequence	2	5	7	×	×	×	0	3
Restored original bit sequence after deinterleaving	0	×	2	3	×	5	×	7

Fig. 2.17 *Block interleaving*

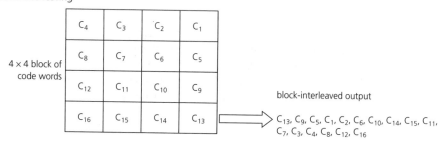

4 × 4 block of code words

block-interleaved output

C_{13}, C_9, C_5, C_1, C_2, C_6, C_{10}, C_{14}, C_{15}, C_{11}, C_7, C_3, C_4, C_8, C_{12}, C_{16}

Convolutional codes invariably outperform block codes, especially for correcting random and burst errors. One of the more efficient algorithms for decoding convolutional codes was devised by *Viterbi*; it produces especially good results in correcting random channel errors. Digital television uses both block coding (Hamming and Reed–Solomon) and convolutional coding.

Interleaving

Many communication systems experience errors in bursts. Correcting an *error burst* is harder than correcting single-bit errors, but interleaving helps to overcome this difficulty. Two types are used in digital television applications: bit interleaving and block or symbol interleaving.

Bit interleaving rearranges the sequence of bits before transmission takes place; its principles are illustrated in Fig. 2.16. Here the order of an 8-bit word (b_0–b_7) is rearranged by interleaving so it becomes b_2, b_5, b_7, b_1, b_4, b_6, b_0, b_3. If after transmission three adjacent bits (b_1, b_4, b_6) went faulty, then deinterleaving at the receiving end would restore the original order of bits and separate the error burst into single-bit errors, which may then be corrected by Hamming, Reed–Solomon or similar coding techniques.

In block interleaving (Fig. 2.17) code words produced by the encoder are written into a memory buffer, row by row: C_1, C_2, C_3, and so on. When the rows have been filled, the code words are transmitted column by column: C_{13}, C_9, C_5, C_1, C_{14}, and so on.

3 Digitising the TV picture

Digital television broadcasting involves transmitting moving pictures as well as stereo-phonic sound. Broadcasting such a high volume of information results in a high speed data stream, which requires a very large bandwidth. But the required bandwidth can be reduced by using data compression. Compression is so effective that more than one programme is made to fit within the existing 8 MHz analogue channel. This is just one of the advantages of digital television broadcasting compared with the traditional ana-logue system. Here are some more:

- Very good picture quality
- Increased number of programmes
- Requires lower transmission power – reduces adjacent channel interference
- Requires lower signal-to-noise ratio
- No ghosting

Figure 3.1 shows the basic elements of a digital television broadcasting system. The analogue video and audio information from the TV camera is first digitized before being compressed to form what is known as a *packetized elementary stream (PES)*. Elementary streams from four, five or even more programmes are multiplexed to form the channel transport stream, which is modulated and transmitted via satellite, terrestrial or cable.

Digitizing a TV picture means sampling the contents of a picture frame, scan-line by scan-line (Fig. 3.2). In order to maintain the quality of the picture, there must be at least as many samples per line as there are pixels, with each sample representing one pixel.

Fig. 3.1 *Basic DTV broadcasting system*

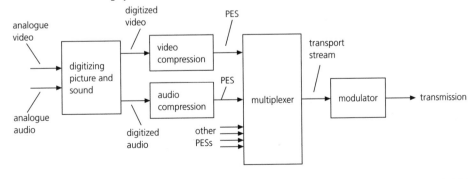

Fig. 3.2 *Video sampling*

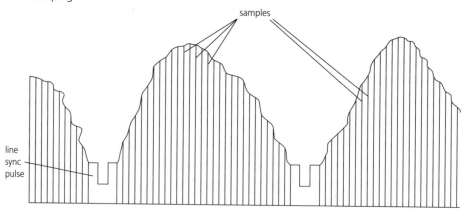

Fig. 3.3 *Line pixels*

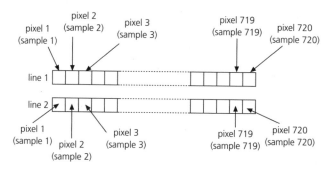

Two factors determine the number of pixels in a television picture: the number of lines per picture and the aspect ratio. As explained in Chapter 1, the British PAL system uses 625 lines, of which 576 are active in that they may be used to carry video information. (For the American 525-line system, the corresponding figure is 480 active lines.) A figure of 5:4 is chosen for the aspect ratio in a digital television; this is to accommodate the process of video encoding, where the picture contents are organized into blocks and macroblocks. If vertical and horizontal resolutions are to be the same, the number of pixels per line may be calculated as

$$576 \times 5/4 = 720$$

Each line will therefore be represented by 720 samples, and each sample will represent one pixel. Sample 1 represents pixel 1, sample 2 represents pixel 2, and so on (Fig. 3.3). The process is then repeated for the second line, and so on until the end of the frame. The process is then repeated all over again for the next frame. To ensure the samples are taken at exactly the same physical point from frame to frame (Fig. 3.4), the sampling frequency must be locked to the line frequency. For this to happen, the sampling rate must be an exact multiple of the line frequency.

The above figures describe what is known as standard definition television (*SDTV*). For high definition television (*HDTV*) the number of pixels per line is increased to 1920

Fig. 3.4 *Samples must be taken at the same point in each frame*

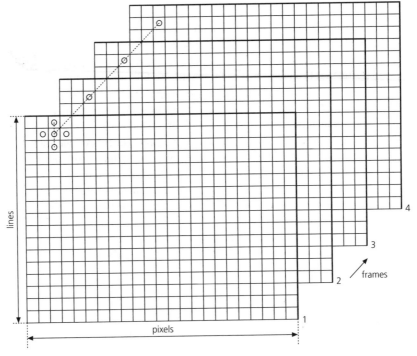

and the number of lines is doubled to 1152, although 1080 lines are normally used with an aspect ratio of 16:9.

Sampling rate

As outlined in Chapter 1, the total period of one line of composite video is 64 μs. Of this, 12 μs is used for the sync pulse, the front porch and the back porch, leaving 52 μs to carry the video information. With 720 pixels per line, we have

$$\text{sampling rate} = \frac{\text{number of pixels per line}}{52} = \frac{720}{52} = 13.8 \text{ MHz}$$

However, since the sampling frequency must also be a whole multiple of the line frequency (to ensure the sampled pixels are in the same physical position in successive frames), a sampling rate of 13.5 MHz (respectively 864 and 858 times the line frequency of the 625 and 525 line broadcasting systems) is recommended by the CCIR (Comité Consultatif International des Radiocommunications).

Recall from Chapter 2 that the sampling frequency must be greater than twice the highest frequency of the analogue input by 10% or more. Thus for the video signal, which at the studio may have a frequency of up to 6 MHz, a sampling rate in excess of $2 \times 6 = 12$ MHz is necessary. The selected rate of 13.5 MHz is therefore quite satisfactory. For high definition television, a sampling frequency of 1920/52 = 36.9 MHz is used.

Video sampling

As outlined in Chapter 1, colour TV broadcasting involves the transmission of three components: luminance Y and colour differences $C_R = R - Y$ and $C_B = B - Y$. In the analogue TV system, the luminance is transmitted directly using amplitude modulation (terrestrial broadcasting) or frequency modulation (satellite broadcasting). The chrominance components are used for quadrature amplitude modulation of a colour subcarrier of 4.43 MHz. The chrominance signals are bandwidth limited to 2.75 MHz, which is far smaller than the bandwidth allocated for the luminance. This is acceptable since the human eye is mainly sensitive to the luminance components of the light wave. The modulated subcarrier is then placed within the luminance bandwidth and transmitted in the normal way. In digital television broadcasting, the three components are first sampled, converted into digital data streams before modulation and subsequent transmission (Fig. 3.5). For the luminance signal, which contains the highest video frequencies, the full sampling rate of 13.5 MHz is used. As for chrominance components C_R and C_B, which contain lower video frequencies, a lower sampling rate is acceptable. The CCIR recommends half the luminance rate, i.e. $0.5 \times 13.5 = 6.75$ MHz. This gives a total sampling rate of $13.5 + 6.75 + 6.75 = 27$ MHz.

4:2:2 sampling structure

There are several structures for subsampling the chrominance components. One way is to sample the chrominance components every other pixel (Fig. 3.6). Known as the 4:2:2 sampling structure, it reduces the chrominance resolution in the horizontal dimension only, leaving the vertical resolution unaffected. The ratio 4:2:2 indicates that both C_R and C_B are sampled at half the rate of the luminance signal. Notice that the chrominance samples are evenly distributed across the picture, producing alternate Y-only columns and alternate co-sited (Y, C_R and C_B) columns. Where interlacing is used, the distribution of the chroma samples remains even in each field (Fig. 3.7).

Fig. 3.5 *Luminance and chrominance sampling*

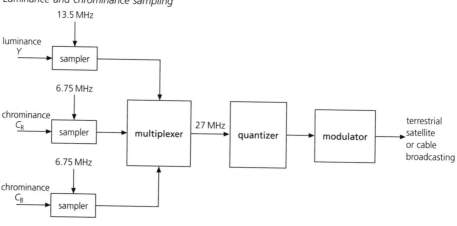

Fig. 3.6 *4:2:2 sampling structure*

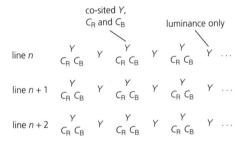

Fig. 3.7 *4:2:2 sampling with interlacing*

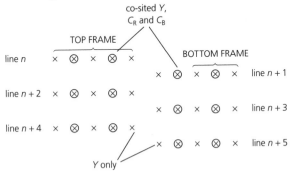

Fig. 3.8 *4:1:1 sampling structure*

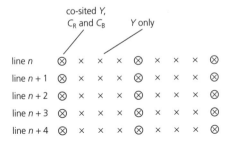

4:2:0 sampling structure

To reduce the bandwidth, and hence lower the bit rate, a 4:1:1 sampling structure may be used. Here the chrominance components are sampled at a quarter of the luminance rate, hence the ratio 4:1:1 (Fig. 3.8). The 4:1:1 sampling structure was used in early digital applications and produced good results. However, it does suffer from a large imbalance between the vertical and horizontal chrominance resolution. To overcome this while keeping the same bit rate, MPEG decided to reduce the chrominance resolution by equal amounts in both the horizontal and vertical dimensions, and that's how 4:2:0 sampling was born. With subsampling in the horizontal and vertical dimensions, the 4:2:0 technique will generate alternate Y-only columns as well as alternate Y-only rows (Fig. 3.9).

Fig. 3.9 *4:2:0 sampling structure*

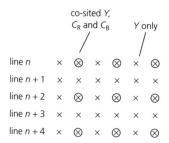

Fig. 3.10 *4:2:0 sampling structure with interlacing*

Fig. 3.11 *Chrominance: simple interpolation*

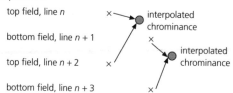

For a sequentially scanned TV picture, chrominance sampling is distributed evenly across the complete TV picture as illustrated in Fig. 3.9. However, if interlacing is introduced (Fig. 3.10) then sampling of the chrominance components will be taken from one field only (the top field) with none taken from the other field (the bottom field). Sample interpolation is used to obtain an even spread of the chroma information. Interpolation involves deducing a single chrominance sample by averaging the chrominance values of two adjacent lines in one field, lines n and $n + 2$ in the top field (Fig. 3.11) and then inserting the sample halfway between two lines, one from the original field, line n top field, and one from the other field, line $n + 1$ bottom field. Similarly, a chrominance sample may be interpolated from lines $n + 2$ and $n + 3$ in the bottom field (Fig. 3.11) to fall between line $n + 2$ top field and line $n + 3$ bottom field. Even distribution of the chrominance samples is therefore achieved when the two fields are combined (Fig. 3.12).

Fig. 3.12 *Combining two fields to achieve even chrominance distribution*

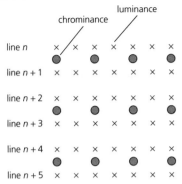

Bit rate

Sampling is followed by the quantization block, where the sample values are rounded up or down to quantum values before they are converted into a multi-bit code. Studio applications use 10-bit coding, but 8-bit coding is regarded as adequate for good quality broadcasting. An 8-bit code provides $2^8 = 256$ discrete signal levels. The bit rate may be calculated as follows:

$$\text{bit rate} = \left(\begin{array}{c}\text{number of samples} \\ \text{per second}\end{array}\right) \times \left(\begin{array}{c}\text{number of bits} \\ \text{per sample}\end{array}\right)$$

But

$$\begin{array}{c}\text{number of samples} \\ \text{per second}\end{array} = \left(\begin{array}{c}\text{number of samples} \\ \text{per picture}\end{array}\right) \times \left(\begin{array}{c}\text{number of pictures} \\ \text{per second}\end{array}\right)$$

And the number of samples per picture

$$720 \times 576 = 414\ 720$$

Then, given a picture rate of 25, we have

$$\begin{array}{c}\text{number of samples} \\ \text{per second}\end{array} = 720 \times 576 \times 25 = 1\ 036\ 800$$

Using an 8-bit code, the bit rate generated by the luminance component is therefore

$$720 \times 576 \times 25 \times 8 = 82\ 944\ 000 = 82.944\ \text{Mbit/s}$$

The bit rate for the chrominance components depends on the chroma subsampling rate, as determined by the sampling structure. For a 4:2:2 sampling structure with horizontal subsampling only, we have

$$\begin{array}{c}\text{number of samples} \\ \text{per picture}\end{array} = 360 \times 576 = 207\ 360$$

This gives a chrominance bit rate of

$$360 \times 576 \times \left(\begin{array}{c}\text{picture} \\ \text{rate}\end{array}\right) \times \left(\begin{array}{c}\text{number of} \\ \text{bits}\end{array}\right) \times \left(\begin{array}{c}\text{number of chrominance} \\ \text{components}\end{array}\right)$$

$$= 360 \times 576 \times 25 \times 8 \times 2 = 82\ 944\ 000 = 82.944 \text{ Mbit/s}$$

Therefore, the total bit rate for 4:2:2 sampling is

$$\left(\begin{array}{c}\text{luminance} \\ \text{bit rate}\end{array}\right) + \left(\begin{array}{c}\text{chrominance} \\ \text{bit rate}\end{array}\right) = (720 \times 576 \times 25 \times 8) + (360 \times 576 \times 25 \times 8 \times 2)$$

$$= 166 \text{ Mbit/s}$$

For a 4:2:0 sampling structure where both horizontal and vertical subsampling are used, the chrominance bit rate is

$$360 \times 288 \times 25 \times 8 \times 2 = 41\ 472\ 000 = 41.472 \text{ Mbit/s}$$

This gives a total bit rate of

$$(720 \times 576 \times 25 \times 8) + (360 \times 288 \times 25 \times 8 \times 2) = 124 \text{ Mbit/s}$$

For HDTV using an 8-bit code, the bit rate generated by the luminance signal is

$$1920 \times 1080 \times 25 \times 8 = 414.7 \text{ Mbit/s}$$

Employing a 4:2:0 sampling structure, the total bit rate becomes 627 Mbit/s.

Bandwidth requirements

A bit rate of 124 Mbit/s (4:2:0 sampling) requires a very wide bandwidth. The precise bandwidth depends on the type of modulation used at the transmitter. For instance, pulse code modulation (PCM) requires a bandwidth of $0.5 \times 124 = 62$ MHz.

The bandwidth may be reduced by employing advanced modulation techniques such as quadrature phase shift keying (QPSK) and quadrature amplitude modulation (QAM). Nonetheless, the bandwidth remains inhibitive for all types of broadcasting media: terrestrial, satellite and cable. Hence the need for data compression and bit reduction techniques. These techniques reduce the number of bits required to define the contents of a picture to a certain level of quality.

Picture quality

The quality of DTV broadcasting is constrained by two main factors: the number of pixels per picture (pixels per line × number of active lines) and the maximum allowable bit rate. Table 3.1 shows the bit rate required for a single programme at different picture qualities and the data compression ratio needed to produce that bit rate.

MPEG-2 defines a number of DTV quality standards by specifying a set of profiles and levels. A profile defines the degree of complexity of the encoding process and the

Table 3.1 *Required bit rate for various picture qualities*

Quality	Bit rate per programme (Mbit/s)	Data compression ratio
Studio	200	no compression
Professional	8–10	25–20
PAL	4–5	50–40
VHS	1–2	200–100

decoding system; a level describes the picture properties such as picture size, resolution and bit rate. MPEG-2 defines six profiles and four levels. Of the 24 possible combinations, only 13 are defined by MPEG (see Appendix A for full details). For entertainment purposes, what is known as standard digital television (SDTV) broadcasting main profile at main level (*MP@ML*) is used. This specifies the maximum bit rate as 15 Mbit/s per channel, the number of pixels as 720×576 and the sampling structure as 4:2:0. MP@HL (main profile at high level) defines HDTV as 1920 pixels per line $\times$ 1152 lines. A more common HDTV application is 1920×1080 lines.

4 Video encoding

A television programme consists of three data components: video, audio and service or domestic data (Fig. 4.1). The original video and audio information is analogue in form and has to be sampled and quantized before being fed into the appropriate encoders. The service or domestic data, which contains additional information such as teletext and network-specific information, is generated in digital form and requires no encoding.

The encoders remove non-essential or redundant parts of the picture and sound signals and perform bit reduction operations to produce individual video and audio data packets, known as the packetized elementary stream (PES). Similarly, service data is also organized into elementary stream packets to form part of the programme PESs. These elementary stream packets are then fed into a multiplexer (MUX) along with the elementary streams of other programmes, to form the transport stream, before going into the modulator for transmission. The choice of modulation is determined by the broadcasting medium: terrestrial, satellite or cable.

Fig. 4.1 *Components of DTV encoding*

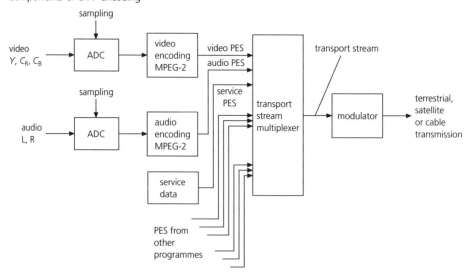

Fig. 4.2 *MPEG-2 video encoding*

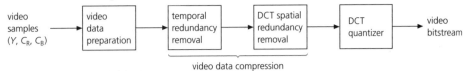

Video encoding consists of three major parts: video data preparation, video data compression and *discrete cosine transform (DCT)* quantization (Fig. 4.2). Video data preparation ensures the raw coded samples of the picture frames are organized in a way that is suitable for data reduction. Video data compression is carried out in accordance with the internationally accepted standards established by the MPEG-2 system. MPEG-2 performs two major data reduction exercises in the following order:

- Temporal (time related, i.e. frame by frame)
- Spatial (space related, i.e. within a frame)

Temporal redundancy removal is an *interframe* data reduction technique which compares 16×16 pixel blocks of two successive picture frames, predicts the difference between them and transmits a vector describing their movement, frame by frame. Spatial redundancy removal, known as *intraframe* compression, removes unnecessary repetitions of the contents of an individual picture frame. It is carried out using a type of Fourier transform known as the *discrete cosine transform*. The purpose of the discrete cosine transform is to transform sample values of an 8×8 block of pixels into coefficients. The number of coefficients is reduced by not transmitting the near-zero coefficients and by quantizing, i.e. rounding up or rounding down to a set containing a smaller number of integer values. Each coefficient is then translated into an 8-bit digital code, which forms the data bitstream.

Video data preparation

The video information enters the video encoder in the form of line-scanned coded samples of luminance Y, and chrominance C_R and C_B. Video preparation involves regrouping these samples into 8×8 blocks to be used in spatial redundancy removal. These blocks are then rearranged into 16×16 *macroblocks* to be used in temporal redundancy removal. The macroblocks are then grouped into slices to be used for further data reduction techniques and resynchronization following error detection. The actual components making up a macroblock are determined by the chosen MPEG-2 profile. Using 4:2:0 sampling, a macroblock will consist of four blocks of luminance and one block of each of the chrominance components C_R and C_B (Fig. 4.3). The macroblocks are then arranged in the order they appear in the picture to form a slice. Theoretically, a slice may range from one macroblock up to the whole picture. But in practice a slice will cover a complete picture row or part of a picture row. The complete picture frame may then be reconstructed by a series of these slices.

Fig. 4.3 *Video data preparation*

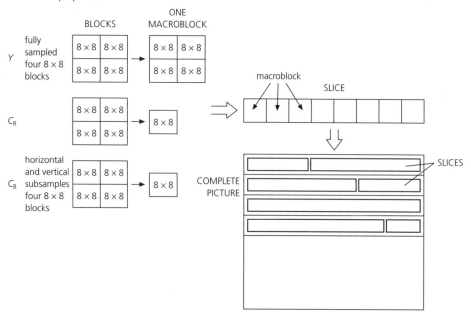

Spatial data compression

The heart of spatial redundancy removal is the *discrete cosine transform (DCT)* processor. Before entering the DCT processor, the line-scanned pixels must be converted into 8 × 8 block scan. The DCT processor thus receives picture frames as a stream of 8 × 8 blocks. The blocks may be part of a luminance frame (Y) or a chrominance frame (C_R or C_B). Sampled values of each block are then fed into the DCT processor (Fig. 4.4), which translates them into an 8 × 8 matrix of DCT coefficients representing the frequency content of the block. The coefficients are then scanned and quantized before transmission.

Fig. 4.4 *Spatial data compression*

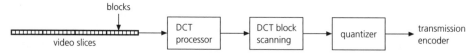

The discrete cosine transform

The discrete cosine transform is a kind of Fourier transform. A transform is a process which takes information in the time domain and expresses it in the frequency domain.

Fig. 4.5 *Fourier transform*

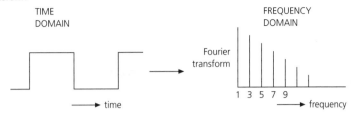

Fig. 4.6 *Analysing a single video frame into two spatial frequency frames: horizontal direction*

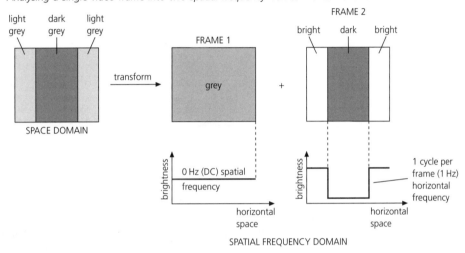

Fourier analysis holds that any time domain waveform can be represented by a series of harmonics (i.e. frequency multiples) of the original fundamental frequency (frequency domain). For instance, the Fourier transform of a 1 kHz square wave is the series of sine waves with frequencies 1 kHz, 3 kHz, 5 kHz, and so on (Fig. 4.5). An inverse Fourier transform is the process of adding these frequency components to convert the information back to the time domain.

In common usage, frequency, measured in hertz, refers to temporal (i.e. time-related) frequency, such as the frequency of audio or video signals. However, frequency need not be restricted to changes over time. Spatial frequency is defined as changes in brightness over the space of a picture frame and can be measured in cycles per frame. The picture frame in Fig. 4.6 can be analysed into two separate spatial frequency frames:

- *Frame 1*: grey throughout the frame representing the average brightness (zero spatial frequency) of the frame.
- *Frame 2*: brightness changing horizontally from bright to dark then back to bright, a horizontal spatial frequency of 1 cycle per frame, equivalent to 1 Hz.

Fig. 4.7 *Analysing a single video frame into two spatial frequency frames: vertical direction*

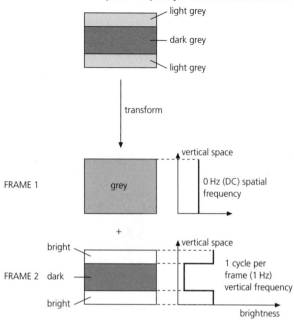

Where changes in brightness occur in the vertical dimension, vertical spatial frequencies are generated (Fig. 4.7). Normal pictures are two-dimensional (2D), and following transformation they will contain diagonal as well as horizontal and vertical spatial frequencies. MPEG-2 specifies DCT as the method of transforming spatial picture frames into spatial frequencies. Each spatial frequency is given a value, known as the DCT coefficient. For an 8 × 8 block of pixel samples, an 8 × 8 block of DCT coefficients is produced (Fig. 4.8). Before DCT the figure in each cell of the 8 × 8 block represents the value of the relevant sample, i.e. the brightness of the pixel represented by the sample. The DCT processor examines the spatial frequency components of the block as a whole and produces an equal number of DCT coefficients to define the contents of the block in the spatial frequency domain.

The top left-hand cell of the DCT block represents the zero spatial frequency, equivalent to 0 Hz or the DC component of temporal frequency. The coefficient in this cell thus represents the average brightness of the block. The coefficients in the other cells represent an increasing spatial frequency component of the block, horizontally, vertically and diagonally. The values of these coefficients are determined by the amount of picture detail within the block.

A block containing identical luminance (or chrominance) throughout, e.g. part of a clear sky, will be represented by the DC component only, with all other coefficients set to zero. A block that contains different picture detail will be represented by various coefficient values in the appropriate cells. Coarse picture detail will utilize a smaller number of cells and the cells will have low coefficients; fine picture detail will utilize a larger number of cells and the cells will have higher coefficients. The block in Fig. 4.9,

Fig. 4.8 *DCT processing*

ORIGINAL BLOCK

146.	144.	149.	153.	155.	155.	155.	155.
150.	151.	153.	156.	159.	156.	156.	156.
155.	155.	160.	163.	158.	156.	156.	156.
163.	161.	162.	160.	160.	159.	159.	159.
159.	160.	161.	162.	162.	155.	155.	155.
161.	161.	161.	161.	160.	157.	157.	157.
161.	162.	161.	163.	162.	157.	157.	157.
160.	162.	161.	161.	163.	158.	158.	158.

DCT BLOCK

314.91	−0.26	−3.02	−1.30	0.53	−0.42	−0.68	0.33
−5.65	−4.37	−1.56	−0.79	−0.71	−0.02	0.11	−0.30
−2.74	−2.32	−0.39	0.38	0.05	−0.24	−0.14	−0.02
−1.77	−0.48	0.06	0.36	0.22	−0.02	−0.01	0.08
−0.16	−0.21	0.37	0.39	−0.03	−0.17	0.15	0.32
0.44	−0.05	0.41	−0.09	−0.19	0.37	0.26	−0.25
−0.32	−0.09	−0.08	−0.37	−0.12	0.43	0.27	−0.19
−0.46	0.39	−0.35	−0.46	0.47	0.30	−0.14	−0.11

The block passes through a DCT processor.

Fig. 4.9 *DCT coefficients of a greyscale display*

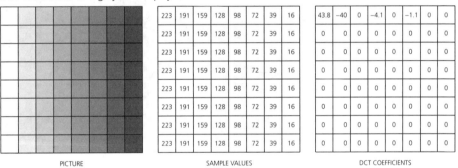

SAMPLE VALUES

223	191	159	128	98	72	39	16
223	191	159	128	98	72	39	16
223	191	159	128	98	72	39	16
223	191	159	128	98	72	39	16
223	191	159	128	98	72	39	16
223	191	159	128	98	72	39	16
223	191	159	128	98	72	39	16
223	191	159	128	98	72	39	16

DCT COEFFICIENTS

43.8	−40	0	−4.1	0	−1.1	0	0
0	0	0	0	0	0	0	0
0	0	0	0	0	0	0	0
0	0	0	0	0	0	0	0
0	0	0	0	0	0	0	0
0	0	0	0	0	0	0	0
0	0	0	0	0	0	0	0
0	0	0	0	0	0	0	0

PICTURE

with decreasing brightness from left to right, has a DC coefficient and horizontal spatial frequency coefficients only.

The spatial frequency represented by each cell may be illustrated by a wave table (Fig. 4.10). The top left-hand cell represents the average brightness. The cells along the horizontal dimension represent horizontal picture detail (horizontal frequency), and vertical detail (vertical frequency) is represented by cells along the vertical dimension. The cell to the right of the DC coefficient represents a spatial frequency of 0.5 cycles per frame followed by spatial frequencies of 1.0 and 1.5 cycles per frame, and so on. Along the vertical dimension, the cell immediately below the DC cell represents a vertical spatial frequency of 0.5 cycles per frame followed by 1.0 and 1.5 cycles per frame, and so on. Other cells represent a combination of horizontal and vertical spatial frequencies. The highest possible spatial frequency, representing the highest possible video detail, is contained in the bottom right-hand cell of the matrix.

Discrete cosine transformation does not directly reduce the number of bits required to represent the 8 × 8 pixel block. Sixty-four pixel sample values are replaced by

Fig. 4.10 *DCT wave table*

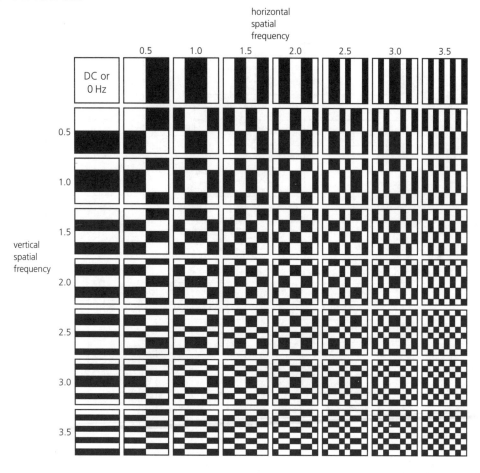

horizontal spatial frequency

vertical spatial frequency

64 DCT coefficient values. The reduction in the number of bits follows from the fact that, for typical blocks of natural images, the distribution of the DCT coefficients is non-uniform. An average DCT matrix has most of its coefficients, and therefore the energy, concentrated at and around the top left-hand corner; the bottom right-hand quadrant has very few coefficients of any substantial value. Bit rate reduction may thus be achieved by not transmitting the zero near-zero coefficients. Further bit reduction may be introduced by weighted quantizing and special coding techniques of the remaining coefficients.

Quantizing the DCT block

After a block has been transformed, the DCT coefficients are quantized (rounded up or down) to a smaller set of possible values to produce a simplified set of coefficients.

Fig. 4.11 *DCT quantization*

314.91	−0.26	−3.02	−1.30	0.53	−0.42	−0.68	0.33
−5.65	−4.37	−1.56	−0.79	−0.71	−0.02	0.11	−0.30
−2.74	−2.32	−0.39	0.38	0.05	−0.24	−0.14	−0.02
−1.77	−0.48	0.06	0.36	0.22	−0.02	−0.01	0.08
−0.16	−0.21	0.37	0.39	−0.03	−0.17	0.15	0.32
0.44	−0.05	0.41	−0.09	−0.19	0.37	0.26	−0.25
−0.32	−0.09	−0.08	−0.37	−0.12	0.43	0.27	−0.19
−0.46	0.39	−0.35	−0.46	0.47	0.30	−0.14	−0.11

315	0	−3	−1	1	0	−1	0
−6	−4	−2	−1	−1	0	0	0
−3	−2	0	0	0	0	0	0
−2	0	0	0	0	0	0	0
0	0	0	0	0	0	0	0
0	0	0	0	0	0	0	0
0	0	0	0	0	0	0	0

For instance, the DCT block in Fig. 4.11 may be reduced to a very few coefficients if a threshold of 1.0 is applied. Further compression is introduced by a non-linear or weighted quantization. The video samples are given a linear quantization but the DCT coefficients receive a non-linear quantization; a different quantization level is applied to each coefficient depending on the spatial frequency it represents within the block. High quantization levels are allocated to coefficients representing low spatial frequencies; this is because the eye is most sensitive to low spatial frequencies. Lower quantization is applied to coefficients representing high spatial frequencies. This will increase the quantization error at these high frequencies, introducing error noise that is irreversible at the receiver. However, these errors are tolerable since high frequency noise is less visible than low frequency noise. The top left-hand coefficient is treated as a special case and is given the highest priority. A more effective weighted quantization may be applied to the chrominance frames since quantization error is less visible in the chrominance components than in the luminance component.

Quantization error is more visible in some blocks than in others; one place where it shows up is in blocks that contain a high contrast edge between two plain areas. Then the quantization parameters can be modified to limit the quantization error, particularly in the high frequency cells.

Zigzag scanning of the DCT matrix

Before coding the quantized coefficients, the DCT matrix is reassembled into a serial stream by scanning each coefficient of the pattern shown in Fig. 4.12, starting at the top left-hand cell (the average brightness component). The zigzag scan pattern makes it more likely that the coefficients having significant values are scanned first followed by the zero coefficients. For the example in Fig. 4.11, the scanned order is 315, 0, −6, −3, −4, −3, −1, −2, −2, 0, 0, 0, −1, 1 and −1. No further transmissions are necessary since the remaining coefficients are zero and thus contain no information. This is indicated by a special *end of block (EOB)* code, appended to the scan. Sometimes a significant

Fig. 4.12 *DCT zigzag scanning: progressively scanned frames*

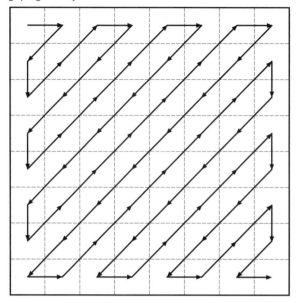

Fig. 4.13 *DCT zigzag scanning: interlaced frames*

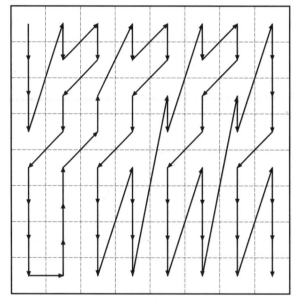

coefficient may be trapped within a block of zeros, then other special codes are used to indicate a long string of zeros.

The zigzag pattern in Fig. 4.12 will optimize the number of successive zero coefficients for a progressively scanned picture frame. A different pattern (Fig. 4.13) has to be used when optimizing the DCT for an interlaced picture scan. This is because, in a field

Fig. 4.14 *(a) Progressive scan: the DCT block is obtained from a screen area 8 lines high. (b) Interlaced scan: the DCT block is obtained from a screen area 16 lines high*

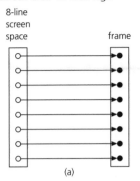

(a)

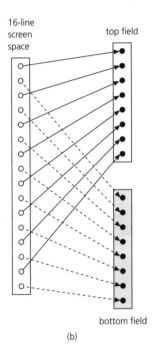

(b)

block, the DCT block contains lines from one field only, and these lines must have come from a screen area of 16 lines high (Fig. 4.14b). In a progressive scan, the DCT block is obtained from a screen area of 8 lines high (Fig. 4.14a). Thus, in the case of an interlaced picture, a DCT coefficient representing a vertical spatial frequency is taken over a vertical dimension that is twice as large as the horizontal dimension (Fig. 4.15). The probability of non-zero or significant vertical frequency coefficients is therefore twice as high as the corresponding probability for horizontal frequencies. Hence the distribution of the interlaced coefficients is different from the distribution of the progressive coefficients. This requires a DCT scan pattern that will favour vertical frequency coefficients twice as much as horizontal frequency coefficients.

Fig. 4.15 *DCT coefficients for an interlaced picture: a DCT coefficient representing a vertical spatial frequency is taken over a vertical dimension twice as large as the horizontal dimension*

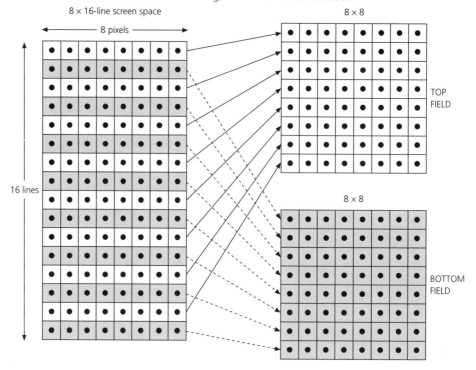

Coding of DCT coefficients

The coding of the quantized DCT coefficients employs two compression techniques: *run-length coding (RLC)* and *variable length coding (VLC)*. Run-length coding exploits the fact that among the non-zero DCT coefficients there are likely to be several successive occurrences of zero coefficients. Instead of transmitting these coefficients as zeros, the number of zero coefficients is encoded as part of the next non-zero coefficient. Consider the following set of DCT values:

12, 6, 0, 4, 3, 0, 0, 5, 7, 0, 0, 0, 0, 0

RLC will form the series of DCT values into the following groups:

(12) (6) (0, 4) (3) (0, 0, 5) (7) (0, 0, 0)

The number of codes required to transmit these values has thus been reduced from 14 to 7 by grouping any zero coefficient or a run of zero coefficients together with the following non-zero coefficient, (0, 4) and (0, 0, 5). Each group is then given a unique code. The final run of zeros is grouped together and replaced by a single end of block (EOB) code. The precise code used for each group is determined by the probability of its occurrence. Those occurring most frequently are given a shorter code word than those that occur infrequently. This is the principle of variable length coding (VLC), also known as *entropy coding*. The most well-known method for variable length coding is the Huffman code, which assumes previous knowledge of the probability of each DCT value. For instance, a DCT value 3 which occurs frequently is allocated a 6-bit code word, namely 0010 10; the infrequent DCT value 12 is allocated a 14-bit code word 0000 0000 1101 00; and a zero followed by a 4 is allocated the 9-bit code word 0010 0001 0. End of block (EOB) is the most frequently occurring string and it is allocated a mere 2-bit code word, namely 10.

The code words are held in a *lookup table* in read-only memory (ROM). At the receiving end, the bitstream has to be resolved into its original code words. To make this possible, the Huffman algorithm ensures that short code words never match the start of any other longer code word, i.e. must not be a prefix of longer code words. For instance, since the code word for EOB is 10, none of the other code words can be prefixed, i.e. start with binary 10. The decoder can then resolve the code words by examining increasing numbers of bits until a match with the lookup table stored in ROM is found. Having deduced the code word, the actual DCT values may then be obtained using another ROM lookup table.

Both RLC and VLC are known as *lossless* coding techniques. Lossless codes, as the name suggests, do not introduce any losses and they are fully reversible at the receiving end.

Buffering

The DCT coefficient quantization, run-length and variable length coding produce a varying bit rate. The actual bit rate depends upon the complexity of the picture content (and the amount and type of motion in the picture). A variable bit rate would occupy a varying amount of bandwidth and may exceed the total available bandwidth with detrimental effect on picture quality. To avoid this, a constant bit rate is obtained by dynamically changing the quantization of the DCT matrix block. (Fig. 4.16). The bitstream is first fed into a memory store before being fed out at a constant rate for transmission. If the bit rate increases, and the buffer begins to overflow, the bit rate control unit is activated; this causes the quantization level to be reduced, thus decreasing the data bit rate. In this way the output of the DCT encoder is kept constant.

The maximum bit rate is a function of the picture quality. For standard definition (SD), main level coding is used which specifies a maximum bit rate of 15 Mbit/s. High definition (HD) broadcasting is limited to 60 Mbit/s or 80 Mbit/s (Table 4.1).

Fig. 4.16 *Buffering to obtain a constant bit rate*

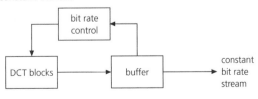

		Table 4.1 *Maximum bit rate is a function of picture quality*		
Level	Frame width (pixels)	Frame height (lines)	Max bit rate (Mbit/s)	Buffer size (KB)
Low	352	288	4	58
Main	**720**	**576**	**15**	**224**
High-1440	1440	1152	60	896
High	1920	1152	80	1194

The DCT coder

Figure 4.17 shows a block diagram of a basic DCT coder. Luminance or chrominance frame pixel values are first converted from line scan to 8×8 block scan before each block is transformed into a DCT matrix of 8×8 coefficients. The coefficients are quantized into a number of quantum levels, determined by the bit rate control, and then scanned to produce a stream of $8 \times 8 = 64$ DCT coefficients for each block. This is followed by run-length and variable length coding. The compressed bitstream is then fed into a RAM buffer to produce a constant bit rate. The final bit rate can be varied by the broadcaster at will. This is carried out by simply adjusting the bit rate control. If the output bit rate is reduced to say VHS quality from standard broadcasting PAL quality, quantization will be coarser and subsequently the picture quality will deteriorate. However, more pro-grammes may then be squeezed into a single RF channel. Conversely, an HDTV channel would demand a much higher bit rate, and hence greater channel space.

Fig. 4.17 *DCT coder*

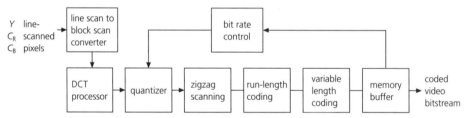

Temporal data compression

Temporal compression, or interframe compression, is carried out before the DCT intra-frame compression. To be exact, both compression techniques form an integrated whole. Temporal compression exploits the fact that the difference between two successive picture frames is very slight. Thus it is not necessary to transmit the full contents of every picture frame since most of it is merely a repetition of the previous frame. Temporal

Fig. 4.18 *P-coded group of pictures*

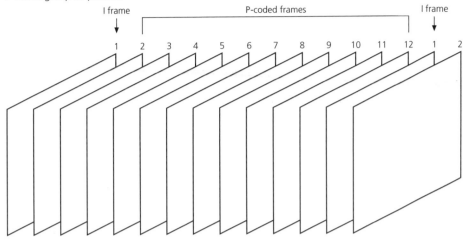

compression is carried out on a *group of pictures (GOP)* composed of 12 non-interlaced frames. The first frame of the group (Fig. 4.18) is known as the I frame (I for inter). The contents of the second frame (immediately following the I frame) are compared with the I frame and a difference frame, known as a P-coded frame, is produced; this P-coded frame is then used for processing. The third frame is then compared with the P-coded frame to produce a new P-coded frame, and so on until the end of the group of 12 picture frames. A new I frame is then produced for the next group of 12 frames, and so on. This is known as forward prediction.

The difference frame could be produced by comparing two frames, pixel by pixel. This would require a very large number of vectors and a consequent increase in bit rate. To avoid this, a *block matching* technique is used. Block matching involves dividing the *Y* component of the reference frame into 16 × 16 pixel macroblocks, taking each macroblock in turn, moving it within a specified area within the next frame and searching for matching pixel values (Fig. 4.19). Although the samples in

Fig. 4.19 *Search area for block matching*

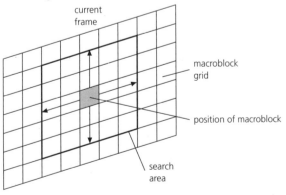

Fig. 4.20 *Block matching to produce motion vector*

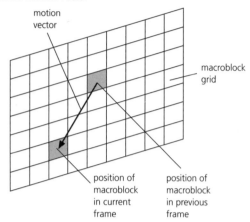

motion
vector

macroblock
grid

position of
macroblock
in current
frame

position of
macroblock
in previous
frame

the macroblock may have changed somewhat, correlation techniques are used to determine the best location match down to one half-pixel. When a match is found, the displacement is then used to obtain a *motion compensation vector* that describes the movement of the macroblock in terms of speed and direction (Fig. 4.20). Only a relatively small amount of data is necessary to describe a motion compensation vector. The actual pixel values of the macroblock themselves do not have to be retransmitted. Once the motion compensation vector has been worked out, it is then used for the other two components, C_R and C_B. Further reductions in bit count are achieved using differential encoding for each motion compensation vector with reference to the previous vector.

The motion compensation vector alone is not sufficient to define the video contents of a picture frame. It may define a moving block but it fails to define any new background that may be revealed by the movement of the block. Further information is therefore necessary. This is obtained by first predicting what a frame (known as a P-coded

Fig. 4.21 *P frame construction using predicted frame decoder*

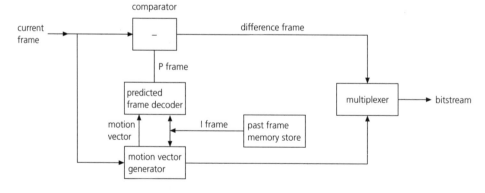

comparator

current
frame

difference frame

P frame

predicted
frame decoder

motion
vector

I frame

past frame
memory store

motion vector
generator

multiplexer

bitstream

Fig. 4.22 *P frame encoding*

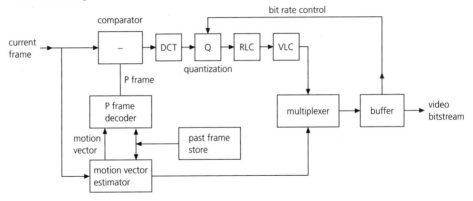

frame normally known as a P frame) would look like if it were reconstructed using only the motion compensation vector and then comparing this with the actual frame. The difference between the two contains the necessary additional information which, together with the motion compensation vector, fully defines the contents of the picture frame. The P frame is constructed using a decoder, identical to the decoder used at the receiving end (Fig. 4.21). The same I frame that was used to generate the motion compensation vector is used to construct the P frame. The P frame is subtracted from the current frame to generate a *difference frame*, which is also known as the *prediction error*. The difference frame is multiplexed with the parameters of the motion compensation vector to form the video bitstream.

The difference frame now consists of a series of spatial pixel sample values, a format suitable for spatial DCT compression. At this stage, spatial DCT compression is applied to each 8 × 8 pixel block of the difference frame (Fig. 4.22). The difference frame is transformed using DCT, dynamic quantization, and RLC/VLC coded before going into the multiplexer. The buffer ensures a constant bit rate.

Encoding the I frame

The I frame is the first frame in the GOP, so unlike the other frames, it cannot be compared with a previous frame. The only type of compression it can accommodate is spatial compression (Fig. 4.23). The incoming I frame bypasses the comparator (pass enabled) to go straight to the DCT, quantization and RLC/VLC processing units. There is no motion compensation vector hence no predicted frame. The generators that produce the motion compensation vector and the P-coded frame are disabled. However, the I frame must be saved to be used in the encoding process of the next frame. This is carried out by the decoder, which performs *inverse quantization* and *inverse DCT (IDCT)* to decompress and reconstruct the frame exactly as it would be reconstructed at the receiving end. Once this has been done and the original I frame has been reconstructed, it is saved in a past frame memory store.

Fig. 4.23 *I frame encoding*

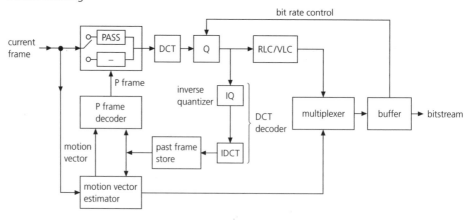

Complete frame codec: forward prediction

P-coded frames in a group of pictures may be obtained by using an I frame or a reconstructed P frame as the reference frame. The past frame memory store must therefore be continually updated as the pictures in the GOP arrive, frame by frame. An MPEG picture coder using forward prediction is shown in Fig. 4.24. The video input, consisting of Y, C_R and C_B pixel sample values, first enters a memory buffer to be fed into the codec, frame by frame as required. Each frame is identified as a Y, a C_R or a C_B as well as an I or P frame in a group of pictures. For the I frame, the pixel samples bypass the comparator and go directly to the DCT encoding section to produce a spatially compressed *DCT frame*.

The quantized DCT coefficients form the only input to the multiplexer since there is no motion compensation vector (or motion vector). The DCT coefficients are also fed

Fig. 4.24 *Forward predicted frame codec*

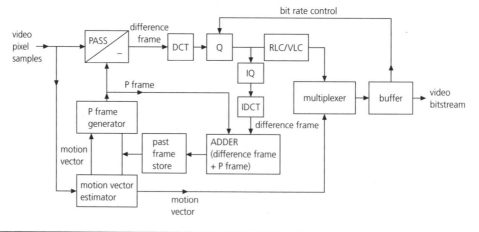

into a DCT decoder to reconstruct the picture back to its original pixel format in exactly the same way as at the receiver. The reconstructed picture frame is the only input to the adder since there is no motion vector generated by the I frame. The reconstructed frame is then saved into the past frame memory store. When the next picture frame arrives, it is first fed into the motion vector generator. At the same time, the I frame stored in the past frame memory is made available to the motion vector generator to produce a motion vector for the frame.

The motion vector is then fed into the P frame generator. At the same time, the saved I frame is made available to the P frame generator. A predicted P frame is therefore produced which takes two separate paths. One path leads to the comparator unit (with subtract selected) to produce a difference frame or prediction error, which after DCT, quantization and RLC/VLC is fed into the multiplexer. The second path takes the P frame to the adder to reconstruct the current (second) picture frame and save it in the past frame memory store to be available for the processing of the next (third) frame. The third frame will follow the same process as the second except that the saved frame, which is used to generate the motion vector and the P frame, is the frame that has been stored in memory during the processing of the previous frame, namely a P-coded picture frame, and so on to the end of the group of pictures.

Bidirectional prediction

The bit rate of the output data stream is highly dependent on the accuracy of the motion vector. A P frame that is predicted from a highly accurate motion vector will be so similar to the actual frame that the difference (prediction error) will be very small, resulting in few data bits and therefore a low bit rate. On the other hand, a highly speculative motion vector will produce a highly inaccurate predictive frame, hence a large frame difference and high bit rate. *Bidirectional prediction* is used to improve the accuracy of the motion vector. This technique relies on the future position of a moving macroblock as well as its previous position.

Bidirectional prediction employs two motion estimators to measure the forward and backward motion vectors, using a past frame and a future frame as the respective anchors. The current frame is simultaneously fed into two motion vector estimators. To produce a forward motion vector, the forward motion estimator takes the current frame and compares it macroblock by macroblock with the past frame that has been saved in the past frame memory store. To produce a backward motion vector, the backward motion estimator takes the current frame and compares it macroblock by macroblock with a future frame that has been saved in the future frame memory store. A third motion vector, an interpolated motion vector, also known as a bidirectional motion vector, may be obtained using the average of the forward and backward motion vectors. Each vector is used to produce three possible predicted frames (Fig. 4.25): P frame, B frame and average or bidirectional frame (Bi frame). These three predicted frames are subtracted from the current frame to produce three prediction errors or difference frames (Fig. 4.26): P, B and Bi difference frames. Following DCT and quantization, the three spatially coded difference frames are compared and the difference frame with the smallest prediction error, i.e. the lowest bit rate, is transmitted (Fig. 4.27).

Fig. 4.25 *Interpolation of a B frame*

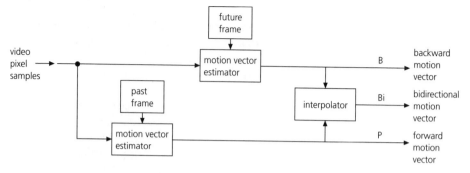

Fig. 4.26 *Production of three difference frames: P, B and Bi*

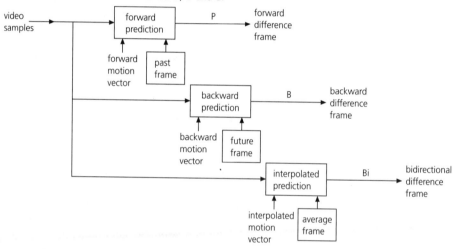

Fig. 4.27 *Transmit the difference frame with the lowest bit rate*

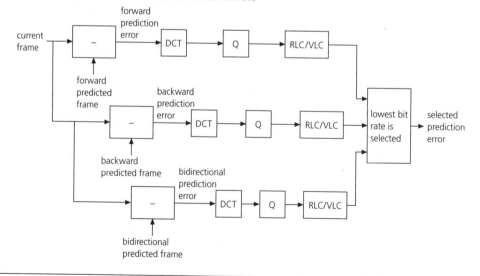

GOP construction

Incoming frames within a group of pictures may be coded in one of three ways: I, P and B. For a given picture quality, a coded I frame needs three times more bits than a coded P frame, which itself requires 50% more bits than a coded Bi frame. For this reason, in a typical group of pictures (GOP) of 12 frames, there are one I frame, three P frames and eight B frames (Fig. 4.28). The composition of the GOP is described with two parameters: the number of pictures in the group and the spacing between anchor frames (I or P frames). For example, Fig. 4.28 shows a GOP with $M = 12$ (12 pictures in the group) and $N = 3$ (an anchor frame I or P occurs every third frame).

In order for the encoder to process a bidirectional frame, the two anchor frames (past and future) must already be available in memory stores. The sequence of the frames must therefore be changed from its natural 'display' order to an encoding 'bitstream' order. Consider the sequence in Fig. 4.29a. The first frame in the GOP is an I frame that will be spatially compressed only and transmitted without a motion vector. The second frame is a B frame. In order to process a B frame, reference must be made to both the preceding I frame, I_1, and the fourth frame, P_4. It is therefore necessary to save P_4 in the future memory store before B_2 is processed. The same applies to the third frame, B_3. For this reason the order of picture frames entering the encoder must be changed to I_1, P_4, B_2, B_3. The same principle applies to B_5 and B_6, which require P_7

Fig. 4.28 *GOP with M = 12 and N = 3*

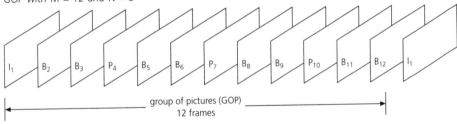

Fig. 4.29 *Take (a) the display order of a group of pictures and rearrange it to produce (b) the order for transmission*

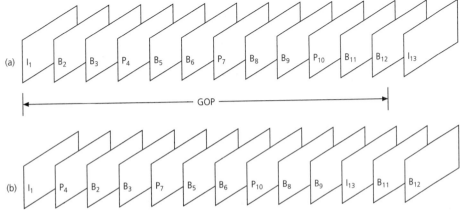

to be available for processing to take place. The sequence of the pictures must therefore be as illustrated in Fig. 4.29b, which forms the order in which the bitstream will be transmitted. At the receiving end, once the bitstream has been decoded, the sequence is rearranged into its natural display order.

Complete video codec

Figure 4.30 shows the elements of a video codec. The incoming sequence of frames are first reordered into a sequence suitable for encoding. A frame that is destined to be an I-coded frame would pass through the comparator, spatial compression and RLC/VLC coding then it would be fed into the buffer to form an output stream. Following spatial encoding, the frame is spatially decoded and saved into the past-frame memory store. A frame that is destined to be a P-coded frame would be fed into the forward motion estimator block to obtain a motion vector. The I frame stored in the past frame memory store is used to predict a P frame and comparing the predicted P frame with the actual frame produces a prediction error frame, which is spatially compressed before being multiplexed with the data representing the motion vector for transmission via the buffer. Following the spatial coding, the prediction error frame is decoded, added to the P frame generated by the forward prediction block to reproduce the original frame and stored into the future-frame memory.

A frame that is destined to be a B-coded frame would be fed into both forward and backward motion estimator blocks, to obtain a forward P vector and a backward B vector. These two vectors are used to produce two predicted frames: a forward predicted frame using the frame stored into the past-frame memory as the anchor frame and a backward predicted frame which uses the frame stored into the future-frame memory as its anchor frame. The two vectors are also averaged to produce an average bidirectional motion vector. This vector is used to produce a third predicted frame, a Bi frame. The three predicted frames are subtracted from their respective current frame and this produces three error prediction frames. The 'select least bit rate' block then examines the bit rate generated by each prediction error and selects the one with the smallest data content. The motion vector associated with the selected frame is then selected to be multiplexed with the prediction error frame. The multiplexed data stream is then fed into the buffer for transmission. Since the B frame is never used as a reference anchor frame, it does not have to be saved and it is therefore discarded.

Differential coding

Further data compression can be achieved using differential coding for the I, P and B frames. In an I frame, the DC component which describes the average brightness of the 8×8 block changes very little between one block and another. A saving in bit rate may thus be achieved if the difference between these blocks is coded instead of their absolute value. Since the difference is likely to be small, fewer bits will be necessary to describe it. The process starts with the first DC coefficient of the slice being sent as an absolute value followed by differential code values to the end of the slice, and so on.

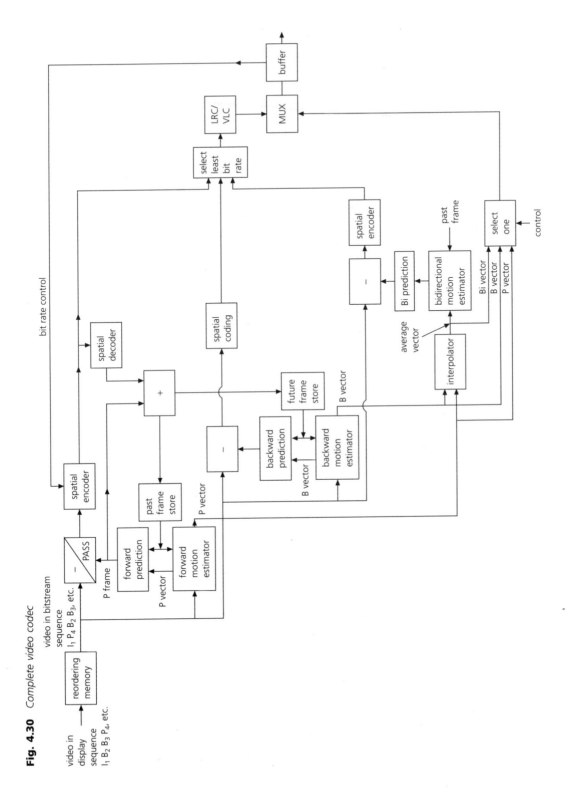

Fig. 4.30 *Complete video codec*

This technique cannot be used for the P or B frames since the DCT blocks represent prediction errors and not actual images, hence their DC components have little relation to each other.

Differential coding can be employed in the coding of the motion vectors obtained by exploring the movement of macroblocks, since in real moving pictures the macroblocks tend to move in the same direction with the same velocity. In this case the first motion vector in a slice is coded in absolute value followed by differential coding for all subsequent vectors to the end of the slice, and so on. Slices are strips of contiguous macroblocks, 16 pixels high. While they vary in size, the sides of the picture must coincide with the start or end of a slice. By making the break-up of the picture into slices dependent on the picture content, the bits required to describe the differential codes may be further reduced. For instance, in a picture of a bright sky it is advantageous for the encoder to have the slices cover the whole width of the picture. However, if half of the picture is dominated by a dark building against a bright sky, then it is advantageous to break the slice into two parts, one covering the dark building and the other covering the bright sky.

Predicting interlaced pictures

One of the main features of MPEG-2 compared with MPEG-1 is its ability to process interlaced pictures used in TV broadcasting. The two fields that form a single frame represent the image at two different times. Where there is little movement, the two fields are almost identical and thus can be combined to form a frame. However, where there is motion, the two fields are increasingly dissimilar with little correlation between them. In this case effective data compression can only take place if the two fields are handled separately. MPEG-2 allows a choice between two basic modes: a field (or interlaced) mode and a frame (or progressive) mode. In the frame mode, the frame is constructed by combining two successive fields.

For spatial DCT encoding, using the frame mode, the blocks to be processed contain lines from both fields. The DCT is thus applied to consecutive points belonging to consecutive fields. These points are separated by a period of 20 ms, giving a field frequency of 50 Hz. Provided there is little movement between successive fields, the DCT coefficients will be very similar to those produced by a progressive scan. However, small amounts of movement from one frame to the next can destroy the correlation between the top and bottom lines, producing too many DCT coefficients. This is avoided by using the field mode, where each macroblock (hence its constituent blocks) contains lines from one field only.

For motion estimation, using the frame mode, a macroblock taken from a top field is used to produce a motion vector and subsequently predict a corresponding macroblock in the next top field. The same holds for bottom fields. The motion vectors thus produced will correspond to a time duration of two fields, 40 ms for a field frequency of 50 Hz. In the field mode, prediction is made using the preceding field giving a motion vector over a duration of one field, 20 ms for a field frequency of 50 Hz. In either case the motion vector is obtained from an area which is 32 pixels high rather than the 16 pixels for progressive scan. The number of vectors in the former case is therefore half the number of vectors in the latter case, creating larger prediction errors at the boundary of

Fig. 4.31 *For picture prediction in interlaced scanning, a 16 × 32 field is divided into two 16 × 8 fields*

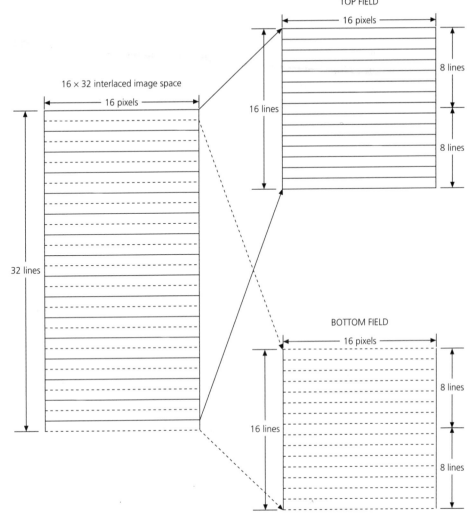

moving objects. For this reason, MPEG-2 has defined a third mode, namely the 16 × 8 mode. This mode restores the vector density, i.e. the number of vectors per complete picture, by dividing the field into two equal parts each of 16 × 8 pixels and producing a separate motion vector for each part (Fig. 4.31).

The dual prime prediction mode

A fourth MPEG-2 prediction mode, the dual prime mode, achieves the same coding efficiency as bidirectional prediction. But unlike bidirectional prediction, which requires picture reordering and hence time delay, the dual prime mode does not employ B frame pictures at all, so it requires no reordering and hence no delay. Two vectors are derived for each field; they generate two predictions which are combined to form the final prediction. For frame pictures, the process is repeated for each of the two fields in the frame. Each field is predicted separately, giving rise to a total of four predictions which are combined to form the final two predictions. The two predictions and their respective motion vectors are transmitted.

For each macroblock, the encoder chooses the mode that results in minimum distortion within the constraints of the available bit rate. The choice of the prediction mode is included in the video elementary stream together with the prediction error, the motion vector and other sync and control data.

Scalable coding

The coding techniques that have been considered so far involve the transmission of a single layer of coded bitstream which is then decoded at the receiving end to reconstruct a picture to a certain quality level. This non-scalable coding is supported by higher profiles and levels. MPEG-2 defines a set of scalable coding schemes which provide two bitstream layers: a lower layer and an upper layer. If the lower layer were decoded alone, a picture with a certain resolution would be produced. However, a high definition decoder would be able to use both layers during decoding and the result would be a high definition picture. There are three main scalable coding schemes: frequency, spatial and signal-to-noise ratio (SNR). In the frequency-scalable coding, the frame is encoded to two different resolutions: a high resolution sent along the upper layer and a low resolution sent along the lower layer. In the spatial type, two predicted pictures are used, one for the lower layer and a second for the upper layer. The lower layer predicted picture is 'upconverted' to enhance the upper layer when full resolution is used. Otherwise, only the lower layer prediction is employed. In the SNR coding scheme, the DCT coefficients are quantized to different levels of accuracy and a low accuracy quantization is sent along the lower layer. To perform a full resolution decoding, both levels are received and the upper level is used to refine the lower-level quantization.

The elementary stream

The output of the video coder is a bitstream known as the video elementary stream (ES). It contains all the necessary information for decoding to take place at the receiver. This information includes the picture information (profile, level, quantizing levels, picture rate, picture size, aspect ratio, type of scan), coding information, programme-specific information including programme identification (PID), and synchronizing data.

5 Audio encoding

Audio encoding has two purposes in digital television broadcasting: to convert analogue audio signals into digital format and to carry out audio compression to reduce the bit rate while maintaining sound quality. Essentially, the system codes only audio signal components that the human ear will hear, and discards any audio information that the ear will not perceive.

MPEG/audio group developed three different standards for audio coding and compression: layers I, II and III. The three levels differ in complexity and performance in terms of bit rate reduction. They are based around two techniques known as MUSICAM (masking pattern sub-band integrated coding and multiplexing) and ASPEC (adaptive spectral perceptual entropy coding). Layer I is a simplified version of MUSICAM which provides low compression rates at low cost. Layer II employs MUSICAM technology in full; it provides high compression rates and is generally employed in DTV broadcasting applications. Layer III combines the best features of both techniques, providing extremely high rates of compression. It is mainly employed in telecommunication applications where high compression ratios are necessary.

Audio masking

It is well known that the human ear can perceive sound frequencies in the range 20 Hz to 20 kHz. However, the sensitivity of the human ear is not linear over the audio frequency range. Experiments show that the human ear has a maximum sensitivity over the range 1–5 kHz and that outside this range its sensitivity decreases. The curve in Fig. 5.1 represents the hearing threshold; sounds below the curve are not perceived by the human ear and they need not be transmitted. However, the hearing threshold will change in the presence of multiple audio signals which could 'mask' the presence of one or more sound signals. There are two types of *audio masking*: spectral (or frequency) masking is where the signals occur simultaneously and *temporal* (i.e. time-related) masking is where the signals occur in close time proximity to each other.

Consider two signals of nearby frequencies, A1 at 500 Hz and A2 at 200 Hz, having the relative loudness shown in Fig. 5.2. Each individual signal is well above the hearing threshold and will be easily perceived by the human ear. But, if they occur simultaneously, the louder sound A2 will tend to mask the softer sound A1, making it less audible or completely inaudible. This is represented by the loud sound A2 shifting the threshold

Fig. 5.1 *Graph showing the sensitivity of the human ear to audio frequencies*

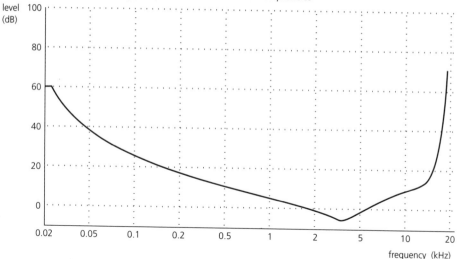

Fig. 5.2 *Nearby frequencies that fall on opposite sides of the masking curve*

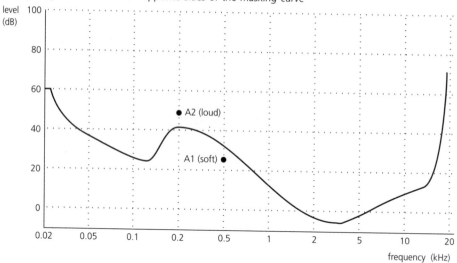

as shown in Fig. 5.2. Two other signals with different frequencies and different relative loudness will result in a different masking shape, and so on.

In temporal masking, a sound of high amplitude will tend to mask sounds immediately preceding it (premasking) and immediately following it (*post-masking*). Temporal masking represents the fact that the ear has a finite time resolution; sounds arriving over a period of about 30 ms are averaged to produce a louder sensation whereas sounds arriving outside that time period are temporally discriminated and perceived separately.

The effects of spectral and temporal masking can be quantified through experimentation to produce a model of human hearing known as a *psycho-acoustical* model. This

Fig. 5.3 *Principles of audio encoding*

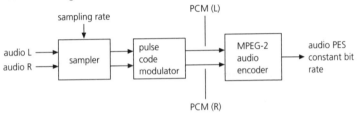

model is then used at the encoding stage to determine which sounds are perceived and therefore need coding and transmitting.

Audio sub-band encoding

The audio signals L and R are digitized before going into the MPEG audio encoder. Digitizing involves sampling the L and R channels separately and then pulse code modulating the samples as shown in Fig. 5.3. The output is a series of PCM pulses representing the audio input. MPEG encoding supports three sampling rates, 32, 44.1 and 48 kHz, any of which may be used by the broadcaster. At this stage, the bit rate could as high as 480 kbit/s per channel depending on the chosen sampling rate; almost 1 Mbit/s is used for hi-fi quality stereophonic sound broadcasting. Audio compression will reduce the bit rate by up to a factor of 7 or 8, depending on the coding layer used. At a sampling frequency of 48 kHz, these are the typical bit rates for hi-fi quality sound:

- Layer I: 192 kbit/s per channel (384 kbit/s for stereo)
- Layer II: 128 kbit/s per channel (256 kbit/s for stereo)
- Layer III: 64 kbit/s per channel (128 kbit/s for stereo)

Encoding itself takes two stages: companding and requantizing. Companding ensures the quantizing noise is kept to a minimum through multiplying low-level sounds by a gain factor. Requantizing is the process of determining the bit allocation to the audio components after all redundant audio components are removed by the masking processor.

MPEG encoding, known as *sub-band encoding*, is applied on fixed-size blocks of audio samples: 384 samples at layer I audio encoding and 1152 samples at layer II encoding. At a sampling rate of 48 kHz, using layer I, 384 samples correspond to an audio time span of $1/48 \times 384 = 8$ ms; whereas using layer II, 1152 samples correspond to a period of $1/48 \times 1152 = 24$ ms. These blocks are further split into 32 frequency sub-bands which become the basic audio encoding blocks. Each sub-band block, known as a *bin*, thus consists of $384/32 = 12$ PCM samples for layer I and $1152/32 = 36$ samples for layer II.

Companding

The purpose of companding is to improve the signal-to-noise ratio (SNR) caused by the quantizing errors; these errors are most pronounced with low-level sounds. Companding is achieved by amplifying or multiplying the samples representing low-level sound by a factor known as the *scale factor*. A scale factor is specified for each sub-band block, or bin, of 12 samples. The amplitudes of the 12 samples are examined and the scale factor is then based on the highest amplitude present in the block. A low scale factor is set where the peak amplitude in the block is high, and vice versa. The small size of the bin (12 samples) is such that the sample amplitudes are unlikely to vary very much. There is a slightly more complex arrangement in layer II coding, where each bin contains 36 samples. The sample with the highest amplitude in the bin is used to set the scale factor for the whole bin. However, if there are vast differences between the amplitudes within each group of 12 samples within the bin, a different scale factor may be set for each 12-sample group. The scale factor is identified by a 6-bit code, giving 64 different levels (0–63). This information is included with the audio packet before transmission.

Requantizing

Once the samples in each sub-band block are companded, they are then requantized in accordance with the predefined masking curve. The principle of MPEG audio masking is based on comparing a spectral analysis of the input signals with a predefined psycho-acoustical masking model to determine the relative importance of each audio component of the input. For any combination of audio frequencies, some components will fall below the masking curve, making them redundant for human hearing. They are discarded and only those components falling above the masking curve are requantized.

A spectral analysis of the input may be derived directly from the 32 sub-bands generated by the filter. This is a crude method which is used at layer I audio encoding. A more accurate analysis of the audio spectrum employed by layer II uses a fast *Fourier transform* (FFT) processor (Fig. 5.4). Once the components that fall below the hearing threshold are removed by the masking processor, the remaining components are allocated appropriate quantizing bits. The masking processor determines the bit allocation for the sub-band block, which is then applied to all samples in the block. Bit allocation is dynamically set with the aim of generating a constant audio bit rate stream over the whole 384-sample or 1152-sample blocks. This means that some sub-bands can have long code words provided others in the same block have shorter code words.

Fig. 5.4 *Sub-band audio encoding*

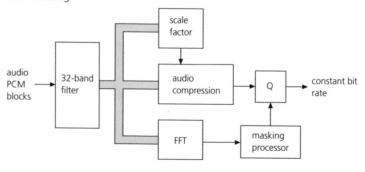

The full layer II audio coder

Analogue audio L and R channels are sampled separately at a predetermined sampling rate. The samples are then encoded as a PCM stream, which is used for MPEG audio encoding (Fig. 5.5). The first stage of the encoding process is to organize the audio PCM stream into basic blocks. This is carried out by first dividing the PCM stream into audio blocks of 1152 samples. These blocks are then filtered into 32 sub-bands, forming 36-sample basic encoding audio blocks. The audio sub-band blocks, or bins, take three different paths: one path examines the individual bins and allocates a companding scale factor to it. A second path feeds the audio blocks into an FFT processor, which prepares a spectral analysis of the input to be used by the threshold masking processor. The masking processor removes redundant audio components and sets the quantizing levels for the remaining audio samples. The companded audio samples are then requantized in accordance with the bit allocation set by the masking threshold processor to generate a fixed bit rate MPEG audio bitstream. Both the scale factor and the bit allocation are varied as necessary to maintain a constant bit rate at the output. The bitstream by itself does not contain sufficient information for the receiving end to decode the audio signals. Information about timing, sampling rate, scale factor and bit allocation has to be included with each MPEG-coded audio block, along with a variety of other data. This information is multiplexed with the audio bitstream to generate an audio elementary stream containing all necessary information for audio decoding at the receiver.

Fig. 5.5 *Layer II MPEG-2 encoder*

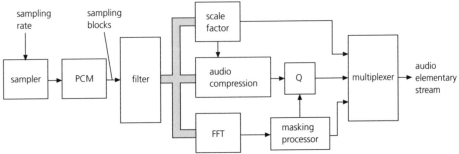

6 MPEG-2 system layer

Video and audio coders deliver their outputs in the form of an elementary stream. Raw uncompressed video or audio data in the form of a digitized picture or digitized audio piece, known as *presentation units*, are fed into their respective coders to produce video and audio access units (Fig. 6.1). A video access unit could be an I, P or B coded picture. The audio access units contain coded information for a few milliseconds of sound (24 ms in the case of audio encoding layer II). The sequence of the access units forms the video and audio elementary streams. Each elementary stream (ES) is then broken up into large portions of packets to form the video or audio packetized elementary stream (PES). Private data and other data are similarly grouped into their own packetized elementary streams. The PES packets are then sliced into smaller transport stream packets. This process is shown in Fig. 6.2.

The transport stream carries data belonging to a number of programmes simultaneously. It is intended for broadcasting applications in which the communication medium is error-prone, be it satellite or terrestrial. An error-prone transmission medium is one that has a potential bit error rate (BER) greater than 10^{-14}. To ensure that errors caused by the transmission medium can be corrected at the receiving end, and to facilitate the multiplexing of several programmes, the transport stream packet is set to a relatively small fixed size of 188 bytes.

For applications on DVD (digital versatile disk or digital video disc), where the communication medium has a lower potential BER, a packet length in kilobytes can be used to form what is known as a programme stream.

Fig. 6.1 *Packetized elementary streams*

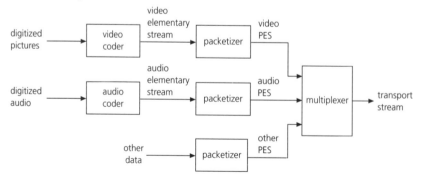

Fig. 6.2 *Turning raw data into transport stream packets*

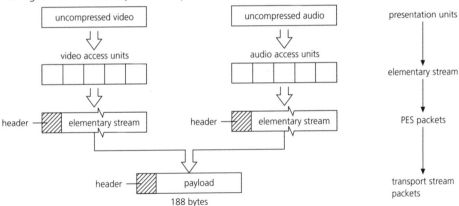

PES packet construction

The PES packet starts with a header followed by a payload, which contains the data (Fig. 6.3). The PES packet may vary in length up to a maximum of 64 KB. A typical length is 2 KB. The payload consists of data bytes taken sequentially from the original elementary stream. There is no requirement to align the start of access units and the start of the payload (Fig. 6.4). Thus a new access unit may start at any point on the payload

Fig. 6.3 *The PES packet*

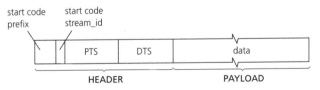

Fig. 6.4 *A single PES packet may contain several small access units*

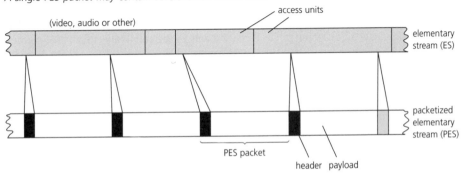

Fig. 6.5 *PES header*

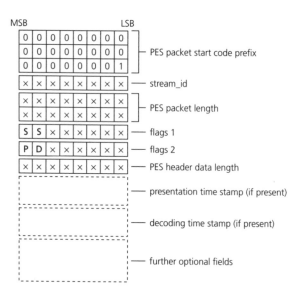

of a PES packet, and it is also possible for several small access units to be contained in a single PES packet. The essential components of the header are the start code prefix (3 bytes), the *start code stream_id* (1 byte), *programme time stamp*, PTS (33 bits) and the decoding time stamp, DTS (33 bits). PTS and DTS need not be included in every PES packet as long as they are included at least once every 100 ms in transport stream applications (DTV) or 700 ms in programme stream applications (DVD). The header includes other fields to define items such as the length of the PES packet, the length of the header itself and whether PTS and DTS fields are present in the packet. Besides these, there are several other optional fields, 25 in total, which may be used to convey additional information about the PES such as whether scrambled or not, relative priority and copyright information.

The MPEG-2 PES packet header fields are 1 byte wide, as illustrated in Fig. 6.5 and outlined in Table 6.1. The first four fields comprise the PES packet start code. It consists of a 24-bit prefix and an 8-bit stream identification (stream_id). This combination of 32 bits is guaranteed not to arise in the packetized elementary stream other than at the start of a PES packet. The prefix is set to 00 00 01 in hex. The stream_id byte distinguishes packets belonging to one elementary stream from those of another within the same programme. MPEG specifies the permitted values for this field, which include 32 different values for audio and 16 different values for video elementary streams. The packet length field is another mandatory field. It indicates the length of the packet in bytes after the end of this field. Two flag fields are provided, flags 1 and flags 2, containing flag bits which show the presence or absence of various optional fields. For instance, the two most significant bits of flags 1, marked SS, indicate the type of scrambling if any, and the two most significant bits of flags 2, marked P and D, indicate the presence or absence of PTS and DTS fields respectively. The last mandatory field, PES_header_length, gives the number of bytes of optional data present in the header before the first byte of the payload is reached.

Table 6.1 *MPEG-2 PES packet header fields*

Field	Description	Number of bits
Start_code_prefix	Code 00 00 01 in hex	24
Stream_id	PES identification code	8
Packet_length	Length of packet in bytes after the end of this field	16
Flags 1	Various flag bits	8
Flags 2	Various flag bits	8
PES_header_length	Length of remaining part of the header	8
Optional	25 optional fields are available	
Stuffing	Bits added to make total number of bits a discrete number of bytes	

Time stamps

At the receiving end, video and audio access units belonging to different programmes arrive at different times. The video and audio access units belonging to the selected programme are fed into a buffer before going into their respective decoders. When instructed to do so, the video decoder takes a complete access unit from the buffer, decodes it and displays the decoded picture on the screen. Similarly, the audio decoder decodes audio access units to provide a few milliseconds of sound to go with the displayed picture. Some kind of time measurement is needed to ensure the video access units are displayed in the correct order and in sync with the audio pieces (*lip-sync*); this is provided by the time stamps. A time stamp is a value representing time; it is generated by the multiplexer at the transmitting end. There are two types of time stamp: *presentation time stamp (PTS)* and *decoding time stamp (DTS)*. The PTS specifies the time when an access unit should be removed from the buffer, decoded and displayed at the receiving end. A PTS is adequate for decoding audio and other data, but a second time stamp is required to decode the video elementary stream; this is the DTS. A DTS specifies the time when a video access unit should be removed from the buffer and decoded but not displayed to the viewer. Instead, the decoded picture is held temporarily in memory for later presentation. This is necessary for I and P coded pictures where they are separated by a B-coded picture. In these cases, both DTS and PTS are necessary. The PTS determines the time when the video access unit is decoded and the DTS determines the time when the decoded picture is released from the temporary store for presentation to the viewer. This means the PTS will always be longer than the DTS. The transfer of data from the buffer and the decoding process itself take a certain amount of time, and this has to be compensated in the design of the decoder.

It is not necessary for every access unit to be allocated a time stamp. A decoder will normally know the rate at which access units are to be decoded and it is therefore sufficient to provide time stamps on an occasional basis to ensure the decoding process maintains long-term synchronization. For DTV broadcasting, MPEG specifies that a time stamp must occur at least every 100 ms in an audio or video PES.

Programme clock reference

For the time stamps to have meaning at the receiving end, some common measure of time must be available. This is provided by the *programme clock* generated at the multiplier stage of the transmitter. The programme clock is based on the 27 MHz video sampling clock. There is no requirement that the system clock should be related to any real-time standard. It is purely a notional time. In the transport stream multiplex, which carries a number of programmes, each programme has its own independent programme clock but it need not be synchronized with the clocks of other programmes, although several programmes may share a single programme clock. Access units are assigned time stamps based on the programme clock. The 27 MHz clock is divided by a factor of 300 to generate a standard time unit of 90 kHz expressed as a 33-bit binary number. Samples of this clock, known as the *programme clock reference (PCR)*, are included in the transport stream. A PCR for each programme clock in the multiplex must appear in the transport stream at least every 100 ms.

At the receiving end, the PCR arriving on the transport stream is used to speed up or slow down the local 27 MHz (36.9 MHz for HDTV) voltage-controlled oscillator. This ensures the two transmitter and receiver clocks are fully synchronized.

In DVD applications the same principles apply except that the clock generated by the encoder is known as the system clock and the 90 kHz samples are called the *system clock reference (SCR)*.

The MPEG-2 transport stream

The MPEG-2 transport stream is a series of 188-byte packets with each packet consisting of a header and a payload. The payload carries data belonging to different PES packets from the various components of one or more programmes. This process is subject to two constraints. The first is that only data from one PES packet may be carried in any one transport packet. The second is that a PES packet should always start at the beginning of the payload part of a transport packet and end at the end of a transport packet. The PES packet itself, typically 2048 KB in length, is larger than the transport packet and will thus be spread across a large number of transport packets. Furthermore, since it is unlikely that a single PES packet will fill the payloads of an integer number of transport packets, the last transport packet that carries the residue of the PES will only be partially occupied (Fig. 6.6). To avoid breaking the two constraints mentioned earlier, the excess space is deliberately 'wasted' by filling it with an adaptation field; the field length is the difference between 184 bytes and the PES residue (Fig. 6.6). This wastage can be minimized through careful choice of PES packet length. It also provides an argument in favour of using long PES packets, as this will ensure that most of the transport packet is filled. The adaptation field is never completely wasted. It is structured so it can carry some useful data such as the PCR (Table 6.2).

Fig. 6.6 *The PES residue is only partially occupied*

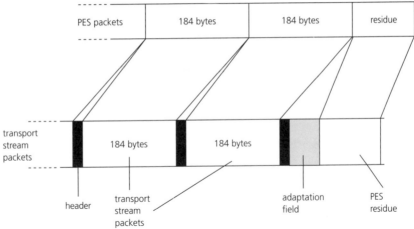

PES packets	184 bytes	184 bytes	residue

transport stream packets

184 bytes | 184 bytes

header

transport stream packets

adaptation field

PES residue

Table 6.2 *The adaptation field is structured to carry some useful data*

Field	Description	Number of bits
Adaptation_field_length	Total length of adaptation field	8
Flags	Various information on subsequent fields	8
Optional fields	Various fields, including a 48-bit PCR field	unspecified
Stuffing	Bytes to fill in reaming space	unspecified

Null transport packets

When all the packetized elementary streams are converted into transport packets, these packets are then sent out sequentially at a constant bit rate to form the MPEG-2 transport stream. The bit rate of the transport stream is determined by the number of transport packets produced by the multiplexer. With few programmes hence fewer packets, the bit rate may fall below the value set by the broadcaster. Then service information and 'null' transport packets are used to soak up any spare multiplex capacity and ensure a constant bit rate.

Transport packet header

Each transport packet comprises a 4-byte header followed by a 184-byte payload of actual video, audio or other data, a total of 188 bytes (Fig. 6.7). The header provides the information needed by the receiver to unpack the various programmes and reproduce the elementary stream of the selected programme. The structure of the transport packet header is illustrated in Fig. 6.8 and listed in Table 6.3.

The header commences with a 1-byte sync word, 01000111 binary (47 hex), which provides a run-in clock sequence for the packet. This sequence is not unique and it can

Fig. 6.7 *Transport stream packet*

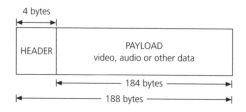

Fig. 6.8 *Transport stream packet header*

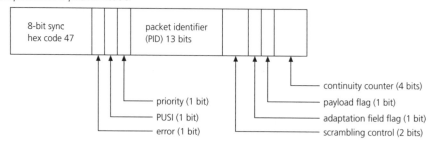

Table 6.3 *Contents of an MPEG-2 transport packet header*

Field	Function	Number of bits
Syn_byte	Header start sequence (hex code 47)	8
Error_indicator	Indicates error in previous stages	1
PUSI	Indicates start of payload	1
Priority	Indicates transport priority	1
PID	Indicates content of packet	13
Scrambling_control	Indicates type of scrambling used	2
Adaptation_field_control	Indicates the presence of an adaptation field	1
Payload flag	Indicates the presence of payload data in the packet	1
Continuity_counter	Keeps count of truncated PES portions	4

PUSI = payload_unit_start_indicator
PID = packet identifier

---

quite naturally occur in other fields of the transport packet. However, the fact that a sync word will occur every 188 bytes within the transport stream enables the decoder to lock onto it. This is another reason for making sure that all payloads are fully filled with actual data or stuffed with useless data. The payload_unit_start_indicator is a 1-bit flag which when set to 1 indicates that the first byte of the payload part of the transport packet is also the first byte of the PES packet. The 13-bit packet identifier (PID) is used to indicate which elementary stream its payload belongs to. There may be many elementary streams comprising many different programmes. With 13 bits there are $2^{13} = 8192$ possible values or codes (0–8191) available to be allocated. Of these, 17 are reserved for special purposes. The remaining 8175 codes may be allocated to elementary streams as necessary. MPEG does not specify any constraints on which PID code of the available 8175 is assigned to which elementary stream, except that elementary streams must be allocated unique PID values. This allocation of PID codes is carried out by the broadcaster at the multiplexer stage. The continuity counter keeps track of how a single PES packet is spread across transport packets. It is incremented between successive transport packets belonging to the same elementary stream.

Programme-specific information

An MPEG transport stream can be used to carry information for more than one programme, where each programme is composed of several elementary streams: audio, video and other data packets. These elementary streams are identified by a unique programme identifier (PID). At the receiving end, the decoder must be able to identify the elementary streams that comprise the selected programme. This is the purpose of the *programme-specific information (PSI)*. Programme-specific information consists of four tables:

- The *programme association table (PAT)* contains a list of all the programmes together with the PID of the transport packets that carry their programme map table (PMT).
- The *programme map table (PMT)* contains a list of all elementary streams belonging to the selected programme with the PIDs of the relevant transport packets.
- The *network information table (NIT)* provides information about the physical network carrying the transport stream, such as channel frequencies and service name; this table is optional.
- The *conditional access table (CAT)* provides information on the scrambling system, if any, and the PID of the transport packets carrying the conditional access management and entitlement information; this table is present only where conditional access is applied.

When a receiver is turned on and a programme selected, the decoder is first directed to the transport packets with a PID of zero to retrieve the PAT. It examines the PAT to identify the PID of the transport packet that contains the PMT for the selected programme. For instance, if programme 1 (BBC) is selected, then from the PAT in Fig. 6.9, PID 306 will be identified and all transport packets with that PID extracted and decoded to produce the PMT for programme 1. The PMT lists the PID of the elementary streams making up the programme and any other private information related to the programme. The next and final step is for the decoder to extract and decode all transport packets with the listed PIDs to reproduce the PES. For programme 1 (Fig. 6.9) that means PID 726 (for the PCR and the video elementary stream), PID 56 (for English language) and PID 585 if subtitles are required. This process naturally takes some time, which

Fig. 6.9 *Programme tables: PAT and PMT*

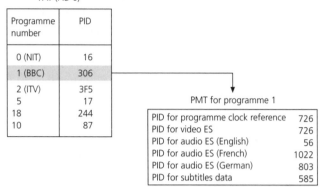

PAT (PID 0)

Programme number	PID
0 (NIT)	16
1 (BBC)	306
2 (ITV)	3F5
5	17
18	244
10	87

PMT for programme 1

PID for programme clock reference	726
PID for video ES	726
PID for audio ES (English)	56
PID for audio ES (French)	1022
PID for audio ES (German)	803
PID for subtitles data	585

explains why changing channels for a digital TV receiver is not as instantaneous as for an analogue TV receiver.

The other two tables, NIT and CAT, are optional. Programme 0 in the PAT is reserved for the NIT, and in Fig. 6.9 it points to PID 16. The CAT is retrieved only if the scramble control flag in the PES header is enabled.

7 Channel encoding

The transport stream emerging from the multiplexer forms what is known as a channel. A DTV channel occupies the same bandwidth as a traditional analogue TV programme but it can carry up to 15 different programmes. Before transmission can take place, the transport stream is first scrambled to obtain an evenly distributed energy across the channel. This is followed by forward error correction before the signal is finally modulated and transmitted (Fig. 7.1).

Fig. 7.1 *Channel encoding*

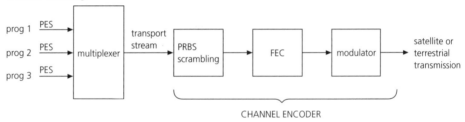

Scrambling

Scrambling is the rearrangement or transposition of the order of the data bits. It is not to be confused with encryption, which is the replacement of the original information by an alternative code pattern. *Encryption* is a secure system and it is used in conditional access applications where programme restriction applies. Scrambling is used only for energy dispersal. In general, however, scrambling is used for both processes and the two terms have become interchangeable.

The problem with plain unscrambled data streams is that they are likely to have long series of 0s and 1s which introduce a DC component; this produces an uneven distribution of energy making the transmission highly inefficient. If the bitstream can be randomized and the series of 0s and 1s scattered, a more even energy distribution will be obtained. This is the purpose of scrambling. Total random scattering is not possible as there is no way of descrambling the bits back to their original order at the receiver. However, a pseudo-random scattering with a known and predictable pattern can be easily descrambled at the receiving end to regenerate the original order of the data bits. This is achieved by using a pseudo-random bit sequencer which produces the same result as totally random distribution. The scrambler consists of a feedback shift register whose output is predictable. At the receiving end, a reciprocal process takes place using a forward shift register, which descrambles the data bits back to their original order. To ensure the start of each transport packet can be recognized, the start byte is not scrambled and the scrambler is disabled for the duration of the start code.

Forward error correction

Digital signals, especially signals with a high level of data compression, require an efficient error protection capability. In digital video broadcasting (DVB) the bit error rate (BER) must be better than 1 in 100 000 million bits (10^{-11}). This is equivalent to less than 1 uncorrected bit in 1 hour of transmission. A transmission channel with such a low BER is known as a *quasi-error-free (QEF)* channel. To accommodate such stringent specifications, preventive measures must be taken to ensure that errors introduced by the physical transmission medium are detected and, where possible, corrected. This is the function of the *forward error correction (FEC)* block. Forward error correction consists of three layers:

- Outer coding
- Interleaving
- Inner coding – for satellite and terrestrial broadcasting only

Outer coding employs the Reed–Solomon code RS(204, 188); this adds 16 bytes to the transport packet, making a total of $188 + 16 = 204$ bytes (Fig. 7.2). It can correct up to eight erroneous bytes in any single transport packet. If the error is higher than 8 bytes, the packet will be marked erroneous and uncorrectable. A code rate of 1/2 is normally used, and this has to be set at the receiver to ensure the signals are properly decoded. Reed–Solomon coding does not provide correction for error bursts, i.e. errors in adjacent bits, hence the need for an interleaving stage.

Interleaving ensures that adjacent bits are separated before transmission. If the transmission medium introduces lengthy bursts of errors, they are broken down at the receiving end by the deinterleaver before reaching the outer decoder.

The *inner layer* employs *convolutional coding* to ensure powerful error correction capabilities at the receiving end. Such error correction capabilities are essential for satellite and terrestrial DTV broadcasting where the medium of transmission is 'error-prone'. This layer is not necessary for a quasi-error-free medium, such as cable in which there is less than one uncorrected error event per hour of transmission.

Fig. 7.2 *The 188-byte transport stream packet and 16-byte FEC*

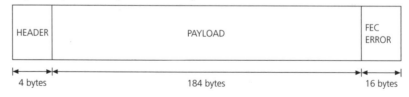

Puncturing

Both inner and outer coding involve the addition of redundancy bits which make code words longer. Long code words increase the bit rate, which in turn increases the potential for errors. These problems may be avoided by shortening the code word, a process known as *puncturing the code*. Puncturing operates by selectively and periodically removing certain coded bits from each code word according to a regular pattern known to the receiver. At the receiver, dummy bits are reinserted to replace the omitted ones, but they are marked as *erasures*, i.e. bits with zero confidence in their accuracy. Consider a code rate of 1/2 that is punctured by removing 1 bit in 4, a puncturing ratio of 1/4. The mother code rate of 1/2 produces 2 coded bits for every 1 uncoded bit and thus 4 coded bits for every 2 uncoded bits. If 1 bit in 4 is punctured, then only 3 coded bits are transmitted for every 2 uncoded bits, which is equivalent to a code rate of 2/3. In fact, this is exactly how a 2/3 rate is generated.

Puncturing a code word increases its code rate as the number of redundant bits is reduced. Punctured codes are obviously less powerful than the original unpunctured mother code. However, there is an acceptable trade-off between performance and code rate as the degree of puncturing increases.

Modulation

The final reduction in the bit rate is provided by the use of advanced modulation techniques. Simple frequency modulation in which logic 0 and logic 1 are represented by two different frequencies is highly inefficient in terms of bit rate and bandwidth requirements. Three types of modulation are used in digital video broadcasting:

- *Differential quadrature phase shift keying (DQPSK)* for DVB satellite (DVB-S)
- *Quadrature amplitude modulation (QAM)* for cable
- *Coded orthogonal frequency division multiplexing (OFDM)* for DVB terrestrial (DVB-T)

Phase shift keying

A digital signal has only two states, 1 and 0, and when it is used to modulate a carrier, only two states of the carrier amplitude, frequency or phase are necessary to convey the digital information. In terms of bandwidth, the most economical form of modulation is phase modulation, known as *phase shift keying (PSK)*. Here the carrier frequency remains constant while its phase changes in discrete quantities in accordance with the logic state of the data bit. Binary PSK (BPSK) is a two-phase modulation technique in which the carrier is transmitted with a reference phase to indicate logic 1 and a phase change of 180° to indicate logic 0.

In quadrature phase shift keying (QPSK), also known as 4-phase PSK, the serial bitstream is first converted into a 2-bit parallel format using a serial-to-parallel converter. The instantaneous states of each pair of bits, known as *dibits*, can take one of four combinations, namely 00, 01, 10 and 11. For each of these combinations the carrier is set

Table 7.1 *QPSK phase angles represent the four 2-bit combinations*	
Phase angle	*Bit combination*
45°	00
135°	01
225°	10
315°	11

Fig. 7.3 *Quadrature PSK (QPSK) encoding phasor diagram*

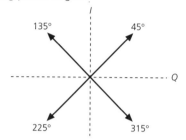

to a particular phase angle. The four 2-bit data combinations are thus represented by four different phase angles (Table 7. 1). The carrier has four phase settings: 45°, 135°, 225° and 315°. For example, data 00 is represented by 45° and 10 is represented by 225°. The four phases are produced by two equal-frequency carriers at right angles to each other (Fig. 7.3): *I (in-phase)* and *Q (quadrature)*. Each phase is used to represent a 2-bit combination known as a *symbol* (Table 7.1). As can be seen, the bit rate is twice the symbol rate (also known as the baud rate). It is the symbol rate, i.e. the rate of phase change, that determines the bandwidth. For the same bandwidth, twice as much information can be sent using QPSK compared with binary PSK.

Differential phase shift keying (DPSK) has no specific reference phase. A phase shift occurs only if the current bit is different from the previous bit. The phase reference is therefore the previously transmitted signal phase. The advantage of this technique is that the receiver and the transmitter do not have to maintain an absolute phase reference with which the phase of the received signal is compared. DQPSK combines the advantages of QPSK and DPSK.

Phase shift keying may be improved by increasing the number of carrier phase angles from 4 in the case of QPSK to 8 or 16 in the case of 8-PSK and 16-PSK respectively. In 8-PSK the carrier may have one of eight different phase angles (Fig. 7.4) with each phasor representing one of eight 3-bit combinations.

Quadrature amplitude modulation

Quadrature amplitude modulation (QAM) is an extension of PSK in that some phasors are changed in amplitude as well as phase to provide increased bit representation. For

Fig. 7.4 *8-PSK encoding phasor diagram*

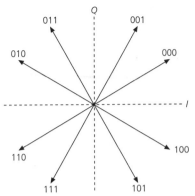

Fig. 7.5 *(a) 16-QAM phasor diagram, (b) 16-QAM constellation map*

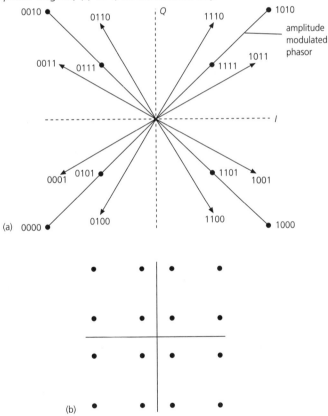

instance, 16-QAM encoding increases the bit width of the modulation to 4 as shown in Fig. 7.5a. Twelve different carrier phasors are used, four of which have two amplitudes to provide further 4-bit combinations. Figure 7.5b depicts all possible carrier phase angles and amplitudes; it is known as a *constellation map*.

Fig. 7.6 *64-QAM constellation map*

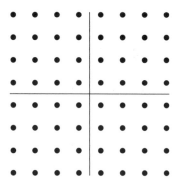

A higher order of digital modulation may be employed, for example, in cable, namely 64-QAM encoding, in which each carrier phase/amplitude represents one of 64 possible 6-bit combinations. The constellation map for 64-QAM is shown in Fig. 7.6.

Orthogonal frequency division multiplexing

Quadrature amplitude modulation encoding is very effective and very efficient. However, unlike satellite transmission, terrestrial broadcasting suffers from multiple path interference (multipath). In terrestrial transmission, besides the direct signal from the transmitter, a receiving aerial may receive one or more signals that have been reflected off tall buildings, trees or moving objects such as flying airplanes. Reflected signals take a longer time to reach the receiving aerial than direct signals, as illustrated in Fig. 7.7. In analogue TV transmission the delayed signal will cause another faded picture to appear on the screen, known as *ghosting*. In digital TV transmission, delayed signals can cause intersymbol interference and fading, which may result in partial or full picture and sound break-up depending on the amount of delay. If the delay is in the region of 180°, the reflected signal cancels out the direct signal and complete picture and sound failure occurs (Fig. 7.8). This can be avoided by using orthogonal frequency division multiplexing (OFDM).

Fig. 7.7 *Delayed analogue TV signal*

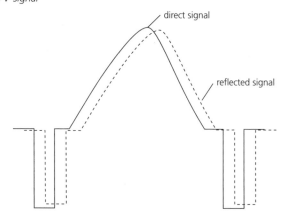

direct signal

reflected signal

Fig. 7.8 *Delayed digital TV signal*

Effect of reflected signals
(a) short symbol duration
(b) long symbol duration (COFDM)

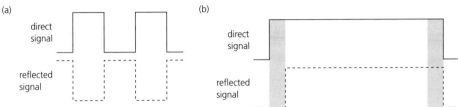

OFDM involves the distribution of a high-rate serial bitstream over a large number of parallel carriers. For each carrier, the bit rate is far below that of the original modulating bitstream. The carriers, 2048 (2K mode) or 8192 (8K mode), are closely and precisely spaced across the available bandwidth. They are modulated (PSK, 16-QAM or 64-QAM) simultaneously at regular intervals with the set of data bits used to modulate the carriers known as the *OFDM symbol*. Due to the large number of carriers, the duration of the OFDM symbol is considerably larger than the duration of one bit of the modulating bitstream. Consider a bitstream consisting of 500 bits, with a bit duration of 0.1 μs. If the 500 bits are used to modulate a single carrier (simple PSK), the duration over which each bit remains 'active', i.e. the symbol duration, is 0.1 μs. If, on the other hand, the 500 bits are used to modulate 500 carriers to form an OFDM symbol, the duration of the OFDM symbol will be $0.1 \times 500 = 50$ μs. With a few thousand carriers and a more efficient modulation, e.g. 6-QAM, the symbol duration could be a few hundred times longer than the duration of the bits in the original bitstream.

With long symbol duration, a reflected signal will only be out of phase with the direct signal for a part of the total duration, shown shaded in Fig. 7.8(b). For the rest of the symbol duration, the reflected signal is actively supporting the direct path signal. To avoid the shaded area, a guard interval (also known as a *guard period*) is added at the start of the symbol during which time the receiver pauses before starting the evaluation of the carriers.

The total symbol duration thus consists of two parts: a useful duration t_u preceded by a guard period set to a fraction of the useful duration, e.g. $t_u/4$, $t_u/8$, $t_u/16$. For instance, employing the 8K mode, the useful symbol duration is set to 896 μs. Using a guard period $t_u/4$ would protect against echoes with delays as large as 224 μs. The introduction of a guard period, however, reduces the number of active carriers available for modulation and hence lowers the data capacity of the system. In the UK the number of carriers used is 2048 but the number of active carriers is only 1705.

In OFDM the carriers are harmonically related with a common and precisely calculated frequency spacing to ensure orthogonality (Fig. 7.9). The spacing is set to the reciprocal of the symbol duration t_u:

OFDM frequency spacing $= 1/t_u$

By ensuring orthogonality of the carriers, the demodulator of one carrier is not made aware of the existence of the other carriers, thus avoiding crosstalk.

Fig. 7.9 *Frequency spectrum for a single OFDM carrier*

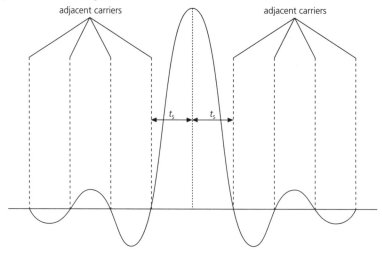

Fig. 7.10 *OFDM frequency spectrum*

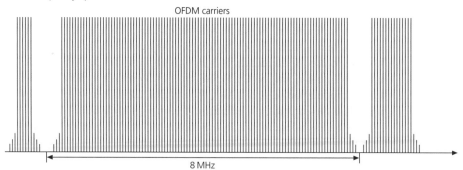

When all the carriers are included, a flat spectrum is obtained (Fig. 7.10); this is designed to occupy the same bandwidth as allocated to a conventional analogue television programme, namely 8 MHz. (It can also be set for 7 or 6 MHz channel bandwidths.) The flat spectrum of OFDM reduces the effective radiated power (ERP) required of the digital terrestrial television (DTTV) transmitter compared with analogue terrestrial broadcasting, in which the carrier power is concentrated in narrow bands around the vision carrier and the colour, FM sound and NICAM subcarriers (Fig. 7.11). In contrast DTTV transmitted power is more evenly and efficiently spread across the whole spectrum, giving considerable savings in power.

Single-frequency network

Apart from improving the quality of reception, the high tolerance to fading and multipath interference has an added advantage. It allows broadcasting authorities to use a single-*frequency network (SFN)* throughout the country. A signal from an adjacent transmitter

Fig. 7.11 *Frequency spectrum for analogue TV transmission*

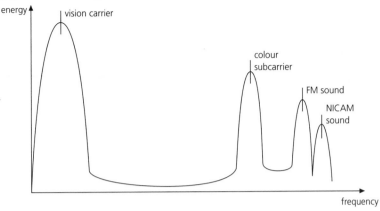

broadcasting an identical signal will cause ghosting in analogue TV transmission. In terrestrial broadcasting, these signals are indistinguishable from reflected waves, and are therefore treated accordingly.

Coded OFDM

Besides multipath interference, terrestrial transmission suffers from frequency-dependent noise caused by narrowband interfering signals within the bandwidth. This is why it is necessary to use a more powerful forward error correction coding system, the C in COFDM, than that used in satellite broadcasting. Noise in the transmission media often causes bits to lose their original logic levels, rather like the erasures introduced by puncturing. At the receiving end, soft decision decoding has to establish whether a received bit is actually logic 1 or logic 0 before an irrevocable decision (hard decision) is taken on its integrity. The process involves gathering information about the effect of noise on all the carriers in the multiplex. A history of possible sequences and their relative likelihood is thus established. Combined with the FEC punctured codes, this history of sequences and their likelihood, known as *channel state information (CSI)* ensures that errors caused by frequency-selective interference and fading are detected and corrected at the receiving end.

8K/2K COFDM modes

For terrestrial digital television, the European DVB (digital video broadcasting) system is based on COFDM modulation with either 8K (8192) or 2K (2048) carriers with a symbol duration t_u of 896 μs and 224 μs respectively. The effective number of carriers, i.e. the actual number of carriers that may be used for COFDM modulation, is 6817 (8K mode) and 1705 (2K mode). The remaining 343 carriers (2K mode) or 1375 carriers (8K mode) are transmitted without any modulation during the guard period. Apart from removing the effect of reflected waves, the guard period performs two other important functions: (a) the carriers that are transmitted during the guard period are used by the decoder for synchronization purposes and (b) the guard period allows the useful carriers

Table 7.2 COFDM specification for 8 MHz bandwidth

Type	8K mode	2K mode
Useful duration t_u (μs)	896	224
Guard interval Δ	$t_u/4,\ t_u/8,\ t_u/16,\ t_u/32$	$t_u/4,\ t_u/8,\ t_u/16,\ t_u/32$
Symbol duration $t_s = t_u + \Delta$		
Number of carriers	8192	2048
Number of active carriers	6817	1705
Carrier spacing $1/t_u$ (Hz)	1116	4464
Spacing between extreme carriers, i.e. bandwidth (MHz)	7.61	7.62

Table 7.3 COFDM specification for 7 MHz bandwidth

Type	8K mode	2K mode
Useful duration t_u (μs)	1024	256
Guard interval Δ	$t_u/4,\ t_u/8,\ t_u/16,\ t_u/32$	$t_u/4,\ t_u/8,\ t_u/16,\ t_u/32$
Symbol duration $t_s = t_u + \Delta$		
Number of carriers	8192	2048
Number of active carriers	6818	1706
Carrier spacing $1/t_u$ (Hz)	976.6	3906
Spacing between extreme carriers (MHz)	6.656	6.656

to settle following the abrupt changes in their phases each time they are modulated by a new set of symbol bits. From among the 1705 carriers (2K system), 1512 are used to carry data. The remaining carriers are used to carry the necessary reference signals for accurate decoding to take place at the receiving end. The 2K COFDM mode is currently used in the UK. However, DTTV being a very flexible broadcasting system, the 8K mode may be introduced in the future without making current decoder boxes redundant. Table 7.2 lists the main characteristics of an OFDM signal for a channel with 8 MHz bandwidth.

The 2K mode provides optimum performance for mobile receivers whereas the 8K mode is generally preferable for large-scale single-frequency networks. The system may be adapted for other channel bandwidths by merely changing the ratio t_u/n, where n is 2048 for the 2K mode and 8192 for the 8K mode. This ratio is known as the *elementary time element*, T, and $1/T$ is known as the *OFDM system clock*. By changing T, hence $1/T$, the characteristics of the emitted signal (apart from the bandwidth) are maintained. For an 8 MHz channel, the system clock is 64/7 MHz while for 7 MHz channels it is modified to 8 MHz. In a 7 MHz channel, the carrier spacing is 976.6 Hz (8K mode) and 3906 Hz (2K mode). Table 7.3 lists OFDM specifications for channels with 7 MHz bandwidth.

The actual bit rate available depends on the type of modulation of the carriers. 64-QAM would result in a 27 Mbit/s multiplex whereas 16-QAM would almost halve the bit rate capacity. However, 64-QAM is more error-prone than 16-QAM. QPSK must be used for DTTV reception on fast-moving vehicles, e.g. trains and cars; this reduces the bit rate capacity to 10–12 Mbit/s but it also reduces the possibility of decoding errors.

Satellite channel encoder

Figure 7.12 shows the main components of a satellite DTV transmission system. The input signal is an MPEG-2 transport stream consisting of 188-byte packets. The signal is first randomized with a pseudo-random bit sequencer for energy dispersal. The Reed–Solomon coding RS(204, 188) adds 16 bytes of error protection data to the packet, making a total of 204 bytes. The error-protected packets are then interleaved before entering the inner coder. The inner coder employs convolutional coding with a mother code rate of 1/2. The convolutional code is then punctured to produce a code rate of 2/3, 3/4, 5/6 or 7/8 as determined by the broadcaster. The error-protected packets are now ready for the QPSK modulator before entering the satellite uplink interface for transmission to the transponder.

Fig. 7.12 *Satellite channel encoder*

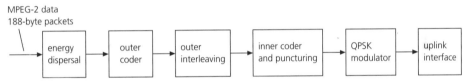

Terrestrial channel encoder

Figure 7.13 shows the main elements of a terrestrial DTV transmission system. The 188-byte MPEG-2 input signal is first randomized and then processed through the inner coder, interleaver and outer coder in the same way as for a satellite system. However, terrestrial DTV broadcasting requires further error protection, provided by the inner interleaver, before the packets can be framed, modulated and transmitted via a UHF aerial. The inner interleaver is a frequency interleaver which carries out bit interleaving as well as symbol interleaving; here 'symbol' refers to the bits being transmitted by one carrier during one OFDM symbol period. The error-protected packet must now be framed before the OFDM modulating stage.

Fig. 7.13 *Terrestrial channel encoder*

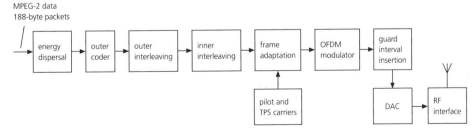

Fig. 7.14 *DVB terrestrial frame*

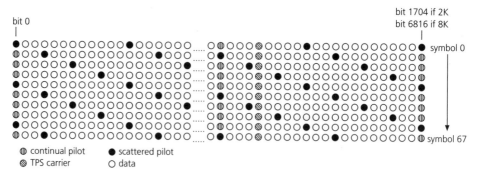

○ continual pilot   ● scattered pilot
◎ TPS carrier   ○ data

A DVB-T frame consist of data from 68 consecutive OFDM symbols together with *reference pilots* and *transmission parameter signalling (TPS)* information scattered among the data (Fig. 7.14). Four OFDM frames constitute one superframe, and one superframe will always carry an integer number of MPEG-2 packets. There are two types of pilot: *continual pilots* and *scattered pilots*. Continual pilots are spread at random over each OFDM symbol. They are used to modulate the same carriers on all OFDM symbols. Scattered pilots are spread evenly in time and frequency across the OFDM symbol. The continual pilots are used for synchronization and phase error estimation whereas the scattered pilots allow the receiver to take account of echoes and other impairments when estimating the channel characteristics. Channel parameters such as mode, guard interval length, modulation type and code rate have to be included within the transmitted bitstream. For this reason, a TPS channel is added to the OFDM signal. The TPS information, 68 bits in length, is carried by specified carriers spread over the entire OFDM frame. One carrier in each symbol is allocated to carry one bit of TPS using simple BPSK (two-phase PSK).

The OFDM modulation is implemented using an inverse FFT where the OFDM carriers (1705 or 6817) are modulated by each frame. The modulation of the carriers may be BPSK (used for TPS channel), 16-QAM or 64-QAM as determined by the broadcaster. The guard interval is added next, followed by a digital-to-analogue converter which prepares the signal for the RF interface.

Hierarchical transmission

Unlike the satellite and cable systems, terrestrial transmission should allow for *two-layer hierarchical systems*. The transmitter in this case will emit two independent MPEG-2 transport streams or layers. The two layers have their own programme data and DVB service information, and they can have different code rates. In hierarchical transmission the MPEG-2 transport stream emanating from the transport multiplexer contains both layers, which have to be split and processed separately for error protection. Hierarchical transmission does not imply any extra complexity at the receiving stage, as only one layer needs to be decoded. The two layers could contain the same programme (with different picture quality) or entirely different programmes.

8 Microprocessing for DTV receivers

The introduction of very large scale integration (*VLSI*) and ultra large scale integration (*ULSI*), with the equivalent of a million or more transistors, paved the way for complex circuits and complete systems on a single silicon chip. A DTV receiver (the set-top box) may contain four types of processor chip:

- General-purpose microprocessors for general system programming and control
- Dedicated microprocessors such as video decoders or transport stream demultiplexers
- Microcontrollers
- System-on-a-chip processors

Three main technologies are employed in the fabrication of integrated circuits: TTL, CMOS and NMOS. CMOS and NMOS are normally used because of their high component density.

General-purpose microprocessor system

Figure 8.1 shows the basic architecture of a microprocessor system. It consists of the following components:

- Central processor unit
- Memory chips (RAM and ROM)
- Address decoder chip
- Input and output interface chips (PIO and UART)
- Direct memory access controller
- Programmable devices
- Bus structure

Central processor unit

The *central processor unit (CPU)* is usually a single VLSI chip containing all the necessary circuitry to interpret and execute program instructions in terms of data manipulation, logic and arithmetic operations, timing and control of the system. The capacity or size of a microprocessor chip is determined by the number of data bits it can handle. An 8-bit processor has an 8-bit data width, a 16-bit chip has a 16-bit data width, and so on.

Fig. 8.1 *Components of a microprocessor-based system*

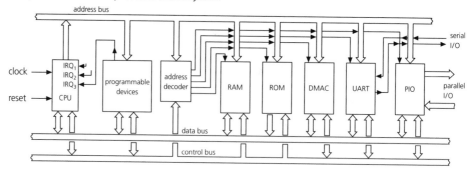

The smaller 8-bit processor is generally employed as a dedicated controller in industrial applications and domestic appliances such as washing machines and TV receivers.

Microprocessors differ in how quickly they execute instructions. CPU speed is indicated by the frequency of the system clock in megahertz. The bit width or size determines the quantity of information that may be transferred in any one cycle, while speed determines the number of these transactions per second.

Memory chips

Microprocessor systems require a certain amount of data storage to hold programs such as start-up routines and other processing software. DRAM (dynamic RAM) and ROM are two types of memory that normally provide this storage space. Other memory, such as PROM, EPROM, EEPROM or flash memory, may also be used.

Address decoder chip

The address decoder receives a group of address lines and depending on their combinations, it enables one of its outputs, normally by taking it to logic low. If this line is connected to the chip select (CS) pin of a memory chip, then that memory chip will be enabled, i.e. selected. With two address lines, four (2^2) outputs are available. With three address lines, eight (2^3) outputs are available, and so on. Figure 8.2 shows a typical 2-to-4 address decoder with its truth table.

Fig. 8.2 *Address decoder and its truth table*

A9	A8	O/P selected
0	0	CS0
0	1	CS1
1	0	CS2
1	1	CS3

Fig. 8.3 *RS-232 connector ports: 9-pin and 25-pin*

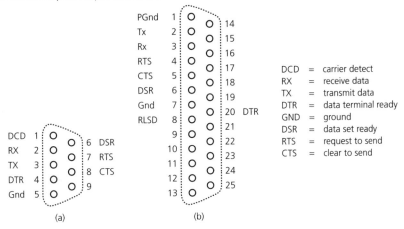

Input/output interface

The input/output (I/O) interface unit connects the system to external devices. It acts as an input or output route for transferring data to and from the peripheral devices such as a keypad, a display unit, a video decoder or remote control infrared signal. Figure 8.1 shows two types of I/O device: PIO and UART. The *PIO (parallel input/output)* provides a parallel communication path to and from the system. The *UART (universal asynchronous receiver/transmitter)* provides a serial communication route with external devices such as modems and mice. The UART provides two data lines, *received data* (RDX or RD) and *transmit data* (TDX or TD), plus several control lines known as *handshake lines*. A standard connector for the UART is the 9-pin or 25-pin RS-232 D-type connector or port (Fig. 8.3).

I/O interface chips are programmable, i.e. they may be used to serve devices with different specifications. A programmable chip has a number of internal *registers*. A register is small data storage, normally 8 bits in length. The mode of operation for the I/O chip is defined by the contents of these registers, which may be altered by the CPU. When an external device such as a modem requests attention, the CPU first initializes the I/O interface, in this case the UART, by loading the appropriate codes in its registers for the specific requirements of the modem such as speed and bit length. When the UART is initialized, the CPU then calls a program known as a service routine, and this allows the system to communicate with the modem.

Direct memory access controller

The vast majority of computer operations involve the transfer of data between different units of the system. The processor itself normally carries this out. Where a large amount of data is to be transferred, a faster method, known as *direct memory access (DMA)*, is normally used and a *DMA controller (DMAC)* takes control of the system for the duration of the transfer. Once the data transfer has been completed, the DMAC returns control to the CPU.

Bus structure

The hardware elements described above are interconnected using a *bus structure*. This structure consists of three bus types: *address bus*, *data bus* and *control bus* (Fig. 8.1). The address and data buses provide a parallel highway along which multi-bit addresses and data travel from one unit to another. The control bus incorporates the lines that carry the control signals to and from the CPU.

The data bus is used to transfer data between the CPU and other elements in the system. The address bus is used to carry the address of memory locations from which data may be retrieved (i.e. read) from memory devices, or to store (i.e. write) data into memory locations. It is also used to address other elements in the system such as the I/O ports. The control bus carries the control signals of the CPU such as the clock, reset, read (RD) and write (WR).

Control signals

The number and type of control signals depend on the microprocessor and the system design. Control signals are normally *active low*, i.e. active when at logic 0. A bar indicates signals that are active low. Here are the main control signals of a CPU.

Clock pulse signal

A clock pulse (Fig. 8.4) is essential to the processor's operation. The clock control signal synchronizes the movement of data around the system and determines its speed of

Fig. 8.4 *Typical clock pulse waveform*

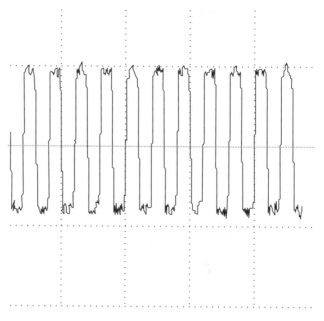

Fig. 8.5 *Typical crystal connection to a microprocessor*

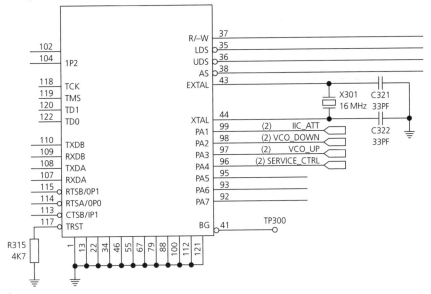

operation; without a clock signal the system would come to a halt. A crystal-controlled oscillator is used to provide accurate and stable timing clock pulses (Fig. 8.5). The oscillator is built into the CPU chip. The frequency of the in-built oscillator is fixed by a crystal connected between pins 43 and 44 (Fig. 8.5) to provide a stable and accurate clock pulse. Clock frequencies vary between the relatively slow 8 MHz to the faster 50 MHz and over. A stable clock frequency is essential and a small drift may cause the processor to malfunction. Clock pulses may be monitored by using a logic probe. To test the accuracy of the clock frequency, a frequency counter or an oscilloscope with appropriate bandwidth may be used.

Read (RD) and write (WR)

The CPU determines the direction of data transfer to or from the microprocessor chip. This is carried out by the read and write control lines. In a read operation, when the CPU is receiving data from memory, the read line is active and allows data to be transferred to the CPU. In a write operation, when the CPU is sending data to memory, the write line is active and enables data transfer from the CPU to memory.

Interrupts

When a peripheral device such as a channel decoder or a transport demultiplexer needs attention, a hardware *interrupt request signal (IRQ)* is sent to the CPU. When such a signal is received, the main program is interrupted temporarily to allow the CPU to deal with the request. After servicing the device, the CPU returns to the original program at the point where it left it. The processor provides one or more interrupt request lines, IRQ1–IRQ3 in Fig. 8.1.

Interrupt request (IRQ) is one type of hardware interrupt where the CPU will complete the current instruction that is being executed before recognizing the interrupt. Other interrupts, such as halt, stop the execution of the main program to allow an external source or device to execute a different program.

Reset

Fig. 8.6 *Simple reset circuit*

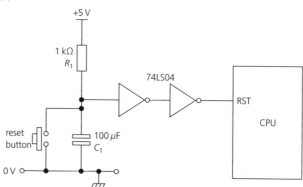

Reset is a type of interrupt which overrides all other interrupts. The reset input pin RST or REST is normally held high. If it is taken low by a manual reset, by accident or by fault, it immediately stops the CPU program, and the processor is reset. To restart the microprocessor operations, the reset pin must be taken high again.

Figure 8.6 shows a press-button manual reset circuit. When power is switched on and 5 V DC supply is established, capacitor C1 charges up through the 1 kΩ resistor. After a short time determined by time constant C_1R_1 (0.1 s), the reset pin goes to logic high and is held there by the 1 kΩ resistor. When that happens, the microprocessor immediately commences an initialization sequence. This sequence consists of directing the CPU to the memory location where the system's start-up program is stored. Two TTL low power Schottky (LS) inverter/buffers (74LS04) are used to ensure the correct logic levels are established. The *RC* network provides a delay, which is needed to avoid *switch bounce*. It is also necessary to ensure that all DC voltages have reached a steady state before the processor is initialized. (A JK flip-flop is sometimes used in place of the simple *RC* circuit.) This simple circuit may be suitable for a system with a single programmable chip such as a CPU. Where a number of programmable chips are involved, as with a digital TV decoder, it requires a more complex reset and initialization circuit.

Resetting and initializing

All programmable chips, including the CPU and power supply control chips, must have their registers set to an initial setting which determines the start-up parameters of the chips. This is known as *initialization*. Initialization involves taking the REST control line from GND to +5 V. Following power on, the simple *RC* network in Fig. 8.6

produces a reset pulse known as *power-on reset (POR)*; this is then used to reset and initialize all programmable chips. The pulse is made active only after the various DC voltages have reached a steady and stable level. This normally requires a delay of 20–60 ms.

The CPU chip

The microprocessor chip has a complex architecture which varies from one manufacturer to another. Here are some principal units:

- Arithmetic and logic unit
- Timing and control logic
- Accumulator and other registers
- Instruction decoder
- Internal bus

General operation

The heart of the system, the microprocessor, operates on a *fetch and execute* cycle. During the *fetch phase*, the CPU receives an instruction from the memory location where the program is stored. The fetch is achieved by the microprocessor placing the address of the appropriate memory location on the address bus and enabling the read control line. The address decoder will select the appropriate memory chip, which places the contents of that location, i.e. the instruction, in the form of a coded binary word on the data bus. The CPU receives the instruction and stores it into an internal register known as the *instruction register*. During the *execute phase*, the CPU decodes the instruction it has received then proceeds to execute it. This is carried out by the CPU generating the necessary timing and control signals for the execution of that particular instruction. The execute phase may involve simple arithmetic operation, e.g. addition and subtraction, or more complex data transfer to or from memory or peripheral devices. Depending on the nature of the instruction, the fetch and execute phases may take more than one clock cycle to complete. When the instruction is completed, the microprocessor then places the next program address on the address bus to commence another fetch and execute cycle.

Timing diagram

The time relationship between the various signals is known as the *timing diagram*. Figure 8.7 shows a typical timing relationship between the clock signal, address, data and read (RD) lines. The clock pulse ensures precise synchronization of address, data and RD control signal. The bits corresponding to the address to be read are placed on the address bus. This is followed by the RD control line going low to enable the reading process. The data is retrieved from memory after one or two clock cycles, when the logic levels on the address bus have had time to settle and the address becomes 'valid'. The process is then repeated for the next read cycle, and so on. Figure 8.8 shows the timing diagram for a write cycle.

Fig. 8.7 *Read cycle*

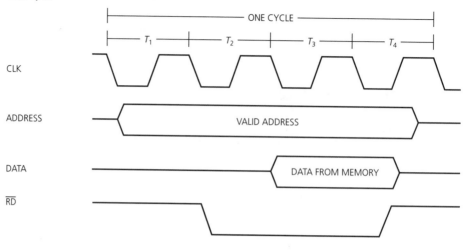

Fig. 8.8 *Write cycle*

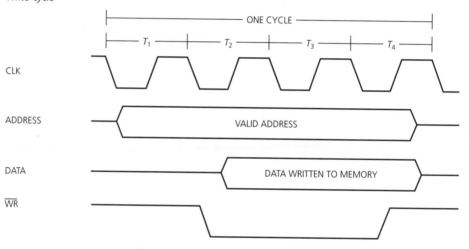

Instruction set

The microprocessor performs its tasks in a predetermined sequence known as the *program*. The program is a series of instructions which breaks down each operation into a number of individual tasks. These instructions are fed into the microprocessor chip in the form of binary digits. An instruction consists of two parts: an *operator* and an *operand*. Each instruction, such as ADD or MOVE DATA, is represented by a binary number known as the *machine code* or *operational code (opcode)*. This is the operator part of the instruction. The other part, the operand, is the data that the opcode will operate on, perhaps two numbers to be added. Assuming an 8-bit system, we will have an 8-bit operator and one or more 8-bit operands. An instruction with several operands takes longer to complete than an instruction with only a few operands. Each make of microprocessor has its own set of machine codes known as the *instruction set*.

Writing programs directly in machine code is a very lengthy and tedious process. Programs are normally written in a language that uses letters and words. This is then translated into the appropriate series of opcodes. The simplest form of translation is the *assembler*, which employs the assembly programming language. In the assembly language each opcode is given a mnemonic such as EN for enable, MOV for move, ANL for logical AND and INC for increment.

Microprocessor types

There are two basic types of microprocessor: *CISC* (complex instruction set code) and the faster *RISC* (reduced instruction set code). RISC processors are capable of performing fast mathematical operations using fewer instructions or a 'reduced' set of instructions. Examples of CISC processors are the Intel 80XXX and Pentium series. Examples of RISC processors are the power PC and OAK.

Single-chip computers

The elements of a microprocessor system (memory, DMA controller, general-purpose input/output (GPIO) ports and a UART) may be incorporated on a single chip to form what is known as a *single-chip computer* (Fig. 8.9). They are used to control *ASICs* (application-specific ICs) or *ASSPs* (application-specific standard purpose) such as analogue video and audio decoders, digital signal processors (DSPs) and digital TV demodulators and demultiplexers.

Fig. 8.9 *Component parts of a single-chip computer*

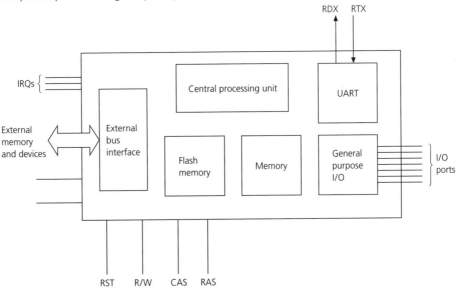

Dedicated processors

Dedicated processors are dedicated to one particular task, e.g. demultiplexing or video/audio decoding. They are programmed and controlled by the resident system processor via the address/data bus and control signals or by a serial bus or both. Processing chips such as demultiplexers and video/audio decoders require their own dedicated memory store, accessed by a dedicated address/data bus. The processor functions in accordance with its own chip clock, which determines the processing speed. This is distinct from the system clock, which provides the necessary system synchronization.

Digital signal processors

Recent advances in microprocessor technology have resulted in the development of very fast *digital signal processor (DSP)* chips. The introduction of faster and denser silicon chips, with the increasing sophistication of processing technology, has led to many applications previously handled by board-level systems being taken over by DSP chips. DSPs can handle intensive amounts of data, carry out very fast data manipulation as well as other functions such as multiplication, digital and analogue concesssion and complex processing algorithms. Available in 16-bit and 24-bit architectures, they are increasingly being used in consumer devices such as CD and DVD players as well as digital TV receivers.

Microcontrollers

Dedicated single-chip computers, microcontrollers are also known as *central control units (CCUs)*. They contain the elements of the microprocessor itself as well as RAM, ROM or other memory devices plus several I/O ports. A variety of microcontrollers are available from various manufacturers (Intel 8048/49 and 8051 series, Motorola 6805 and 146805, Texas TMS1000 and Zilog Z80 series) for use as dedicated computer systems in applications such as car engines, washing machines, VCRs and of course TV receivers. The difference between one type of microprocessor and another lies in the type and size of memory, instruction set, operating speed, number of available I/O lines and data width (e.g. 4, 8 or 16 bits). Most microcontrollers have their program stored permanently into internal ROM at the manufacturing stage, a process known as *mask programming*. Some chips have an external EPROM for user programming.

Internal architecture

Figure 8.10 shows the basic architecture of an 8-bit minicontroller. The program is held in ROM with a small RAM of 1–4 KB available for data and other external control signals. The timer/counter may be loaded, started, stopped or read by software commands. In TV applications it tracks the sequence of lines and fields and prompts the controller to carry out certain operations at specific times. Figure 8.10 shows one parallel 8-bit port (port A). Each port may be assigned as an input or an output. A serial I/O port may be established by using two lines of the parallel ports, one to receive and the other to transmit serial data. The chip also supports a serial bus, which is used to control peripheral devices such as tuners and demodulators. The arithmetic and logic unit (ALU)

Fig. 8.10 *Microcontroller internal architecture*

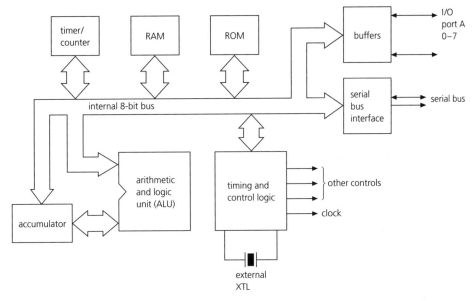

carries out arithmetic operations such as adding two numbers; it also performs logic functions such as NAND or NOR on two numbers. The ALU therefore has two inputs, one input for each number. When the ALU operation is completed, the result is stored in the accumulator. The timing and control unit provides the necessary synchronization of the system through the clock and other control signals. A single multiplexed 8-bit bus provides interconnection between the various units. Figure 8.11 shows a typical micro-controller chip used in receivers.

Fig. 8.11 *Typical TV receiver microcontroller*

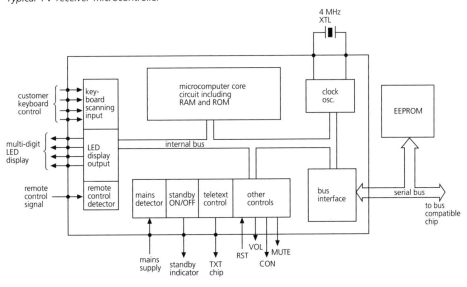

Fig. 8.12 *Two-line I²C serial control bus*

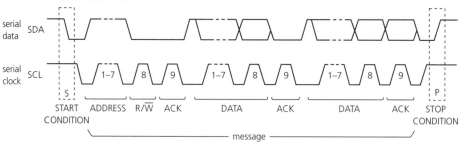

Serial control bus

Microcontrollers use a serial bus to control other devices. There are two main types of serial control bus: the two-line *inter IC bus (IIC or I²C)* and the three-line *Intermetall bus (IM)*. The I²C bus has two bidirectional lines, a serial clock (*SCL*) and serial data (*SDA*). Any unit connected to the bus may send and receive data. Data is transmitted in 8-bit words or bytes (Fig. 8.12). The first byte contains the 7-bit address of the device for which the information is intended, and the eighth bit is a read/write bit to signify whether the data is required from or being sent to the device. A number of data bytes follow. The total number in a message depends on the nature of information being transferred. Each data byte is terminated by an acknowledge (*ACK*) bit. Like all other bits, the ACK bit has a related clock pulse on the clock line as shown.

The first byte of any data transfer is preceded by a start condition and is terminated by a stop condition. An arbitration logic system is used to ensure that two devices do not use the bus simultaneously. The clock has a variable speed and operates only when data is transferred. Data may be sent at a slow rate or a fast rate of up to 100 kbit/s.

The Intermetall bus has three lines, ident (I), clock (C) and data (D). The ident and clock lines are unidirectional between the microcontroller and the other peripheral devices; the data line is bidirectional. The start of transmission is indicated by the ident line going low (Fig. 8.13). An 8-bit address is sent along the data line. At the end of eight clock cycles, the I line goes high to indicate the start of data transmission. Data is then transmitted along the D line for 8 (16) clock cycles for an 8-bit (16-bit) data word, after which the I line goes low again to indicate the end of data transmission.

Both buses may be used simultaneously in a single receiver to provide connections with different sections of the receiver. A number of peripheral chips are available in the market, including tuner interfaces, channel decoders, EEPROMs, ADCs and a variety of DSPs for operation with I²C or IM buses.

A serial bus may be tested by using a logic probe or an oscilloscope to test for a pulse train. However, care must be taken to ensure that a signal is being sent along the serial lines when the test is being carried out. This is easily achieved by activating the remote control.

Fig. 8.13 *Three-line Intermetall serial control bus*

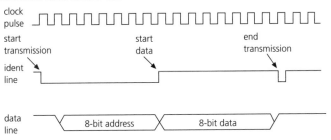

System-on-a-chip

Evolution in chip technology has vastly increased the density of integrated circuits and their functionality. Changing from a 0.5 μm integrated circuit technology to 0.18 μm has resulted in a vast unused space known as *white space* (Fig. 8.14), which may be utilized for extra functions. This space is used to perform various processes (analogue or digital) as well as providing DRAM, SRAM, EPROM or flash embedded memories. Merging different processes in this way produces a single universal process. This type of processor is called *system-on-a-chip (SoC)*.

Fig. 8.14 *New IC technology has led to vast amounts of unused 'white' space*

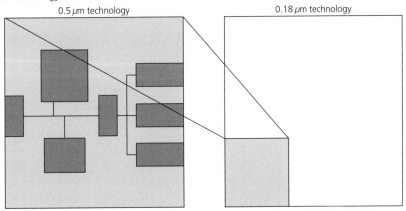

System-on-a-chip is the latest advance in chip technology and is likely to replace ASICs in the next few years. SoC combines a CPU core with an application block together with embedded memory space (DRAM, SRAM or flash), I/O ports, serial UART and external bus interface (Fig. 8.15). A special interface is usually provided for use during testing and development. The core is based on a powerful RISC processor chip such as the ARM or OAK families. SoC processors carry out two functions simultaneously:

Fig. 8.15 *System-on-a-chip*

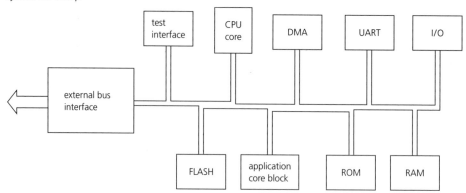

- They program and control external devices (such as video/audio decoders and terrestrial DTV demodulators) using their powerful CPU core.
- They carry out a specific complex processing operation such as transport demultiplexing in a DTV decoder.

In short, SoC doubles as a general-purpose processor and a dedicated processor.

9 The integrated receiver decoder front end

Digital TV reception is normally provided by an *integrated receiver decoder (IRD)* commonly known as a set-top box (*STB*). The IRD tunes to the required channel, extracts and decodes the selected programme data, checks the access rights of the user and produces picture, sound and other services as needed.

Digital signals are fed to the IRD in the same way as for analogue TV broadcasting. Thus, in the case of satellite transmission, an outdoor dish and low noise block (*LNB*) are necessary to receive the signals and convert them to a suitable intermediate frequency (IF). For terrestrial television, the input to the IRD is obtained directly from a terrestrial aerial. And for cable too, the signal is obtained directly from the network. The output from the IRD, in the form of analogue video and audio signals, is fed to an analogue TV receiver either directly via a *SCART* connection or as a UHF-modulated signal using the aerial socket at the back of the receiver (Fig. 9.1).

Fig. 9.1 *UHF and SCART connections between set-top box and TV receiver*

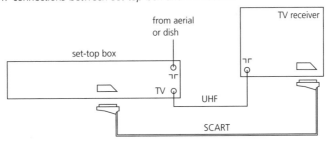

System overview

Figure 9.2 shows the basic components of a DTV IRD. The front end, which is specific to the broadcasting media, converts the input signals (RF for terrestrial or IF for satellite and cable broadcasting) to an MPEG transport stream. It consists of a tuner, ADC and a channel decoder which includes a demodulator and a forward error correction (FEC) processor. The transport stream containing standard 204-byte packets belonging to one or more television programmes is fed into the transport demultiplexer. Before processing the transport stream, the demultiplexer sends the bitstream to the conditional access

Fig. 9.2 *Components of a DTV integrated receiver/decoder*

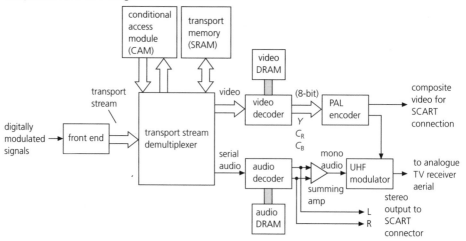

module (CAM), which controls the user access rights to the selected service. The CAM interrogates a smart card to find out if the user has a current subscription to the selected programme. If access is granted, the transport stream is routed back into the transport demultiplxer. The demultiplexer selects the transport packets belonging to the chosen programme and reassembles them to reconstruct the packetized elementary streams of the programme. Two sets of digital signals are produced by the transport demultiplexer – an 8-bit wide video output and a serial audio output – which are fed to their respective decoders. A fast SRAM (static RAM) is used to buffer the video and audio data so that onward transmission to the video and audio decoders can take place in bursts.

The video section consists of an MPEG-2 video decoder which decompresses the video data stream and converts it back into its original components: Y (luminance) and C_R and C_B (chrominance). The picture is reconstructed from the I, P and B frames. This reconstruction requires simultaneous storage of these frames, hence the need for a large video memory in the form of a DRAM buffer, or a faster synchronous DRAM (SDRAM) buffer. The three components are sent to the PAL encoder to convert the digital video into an analogue PAL composite video, which is fed directly to a television set via a SCART connector or into a UHF modulator as shown.

The audio section consists of an MPEG-2 audio decoder. Here the audio packets are decoded using the same rules as adopted in the encoding stage to produce left and right analogue audio signals. Audio buffering is provided by an audio DRAM memory chip, which among other things provides a 1 s delay to ensure audio and video synchronization. This delay is necessary given that the processing of the video signals takes a longer time to be completed than the processing of audio signals. The left and right analogue audio signals from the audio decoder are fed into a summing amplifier to produce mono sound for the UHF modulator. A separate stereo output (L and R) is also provided, and this may be sent to a television set via a SCART connector.

The UHF modulator combines the video and mono audio signals and modulates them on a UHF frequency in the same way as a traditional analogue transmitter. The modulated UHF is then fed into the aerial socket of the television set. The modulator section will also include a loop-through facility for analogue broadcasts from a terrestrial aerial to be fed to the TV set.

Programming and control

The system requires a high level of programming and control. This is performed by a 16-bit or a 32-bit host microprocessor (Fig. 9.3). Control is exercised using normal control signals such as read/write, reset and interrupt request (IRQ) as well as a serial bus such as the I²C control bus. The microprocessor system also carries out the necessary software programming and control of all the units.

Fig. 9.3 *IRD control system*

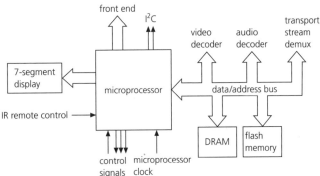

The host microprocessor controls the audio and video decoding, the transport stream demultiplexer and the conditional access module, and it runs the receiver menu system. It has its own clock, its own address, data and control bus structure, and its own DRAM and flash memory stores. The non-volatile flash memory chip is used to store software programs used in the decoding process. Upgrading of the software may be carried out off-air by first loading the new software into the DRAM chips and then transferring it to the non-volatile flash memory. Furthermore, the microprocessor monitors the power supply, decodes the infrared information from the remote control handset and front panel buttons, controls the tuner, controls the channel decoder including the demodulator and the FEC processor, and configures and controls the PAL decoder.

The front end

The function of the front end of a DVB set-top box is to extract the multiplexed transport stream from the modulated carrier received from a satellite dish or a terrestrial aerial. There are four stages (Fig. 9.4):

- A tuner stage
- An analogue-to-digital converter
- A demodulator: QPSK for satellite reception; OFDM for terrestrial reception
- An FEC decoder to detect and correct errors

Fig. 9.4 *The front end*

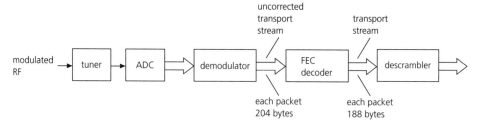

The precise construction of the front end depends on the type of receiver, satellite or terrestrial. For cable digital video broadcasting (DVB-C), the front end is similar to that used for satellite reception except for the input carrier frequency.

DVB satellite front end

Figure 9.5 shows the basic components of a satellite DTV receiver front end. The tuner is a self-contained isolated unit. The input to the tuner is in the form of a carrier known as the first IF from the low noise block (LNB) of a satellite dish. It is frequency modulated by a signal, itself a QPSK-modulated carrier. The tuner downconverts the input carrier to a second IF and reproduces the two original QPSK-modulated carrier signals: in-phase (I) and quadrature (Q). The phase-modulated I and Q carriers have the distinctive waveform shown in Fig. 9.6.

Fig. 9.5 *Front end: satellite*

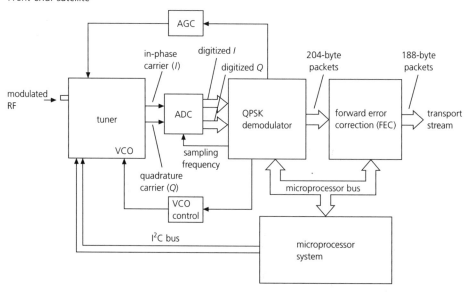

Fig. 9.6 *Typical I or Q carrier waveform*

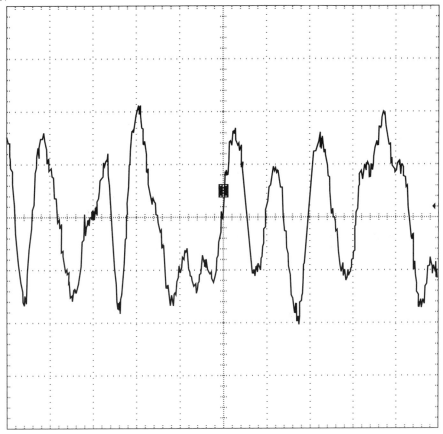

The *I* and *Q* carriers are fed into a dual ADC (one for each carrier), which converts them into two 6-bit digital signals. The sampling rate is set by a signal from the QPSK demodulator, which controls an in-built VCO. The sampling rate is normally set to twice the symbol rate, i.e. the rate at which the phase of the carrier changes. The symbol rate itself is determined by the broadcaster and has to be set at the receiver before the tuner can select a channel. Thus, for a symbol rate of 27 500 kilosymbols per second, the sampling rate will be set at $2 \times 27.5 = 55$ MHz (not to be confused with the 27 MHz video sampling rate). Where the symbol rate is low, a sampling rate of three times the symbol rate is usually used. Cable broadcasting uses a sampling rate of four times the symbol rate.

The recovery of the original transport stream from the *I* and *Q* carriers involves two distinct stages, *phase recovery* and *data recovery*. Phase recovery identifies the phase change of the carrier; data recovery reproduces the original bitstream, a process known as symbol-to-bit mapping. The QPSK demodulator carries out phase recovery whereas data recovery is incorporated within the FEC chip. The demodulator carries out the phase detection of the *I* and *Q* signals, samples the recovered phases and quantizes each phase

Fig. 9.7 *FEC error detection/correction stage*

204-byte packets → Viterbi decoder → deinterleaver → RS decoder → 188-byte packets

change into a 3-bit coded output. The demodulator normally carries out several other functions:

- It estimates the input signal power and provides an automatic gain control (AGC) control signal to the tuner, The purpose of the AGC is to control the gain of the tuner so the tuner's output remains constant as its input changes.
- It provides a synchronizing signal for the tuner local oscillator via the VCO control line.
- It provides the dual ADC with the required sampling rate either directly or more commonly via a control signal to an in-built VCO or numerically controlled oscillator.

The digitized I and Q signals from the demodulator are then fed into the FEC decoder. The FEC decoder first recovers the modulating data bits from the QPSK carriers and arranges the information in a way that is suitable for presentation to the error detection/correction stage. The FEC error detection/correction stage consists of three parts (Fig. 9.7). First comes the Viterbi decoder, which uses the original convolutional coding to determine whether a received bit is a logic 0 or a logic 1. Next comes the deinterleaver. Following the soft decision making of the Viterbi decoder, it rearranges the symbols and bits into the order they had before they were interleaved at the transmitting stage. The final part is the Reed–Solomon (RS) decoder, which performs the hard decisions. Hard decisions determine whether a packet contains errors. If it does, the FEC unit will attempt to correct them. Failing that, the FEC decoder will flag the packet that contains errors so it may not be used in subsequent processing. At the end of the process, the result is a transport stream that consists of a series of 188-byte transport packets. Before the transport packets are fed to the demultiplexer for further processing, the pseudo-random energy dispersal is removed by a descrambler using the reverse of algorithms applied during transmission.

DTV front ends are fully programmable and controllable by the system host microprocessor. The tuner is normally controlled by a serial bus such as the I²C bus. The demodulator and the FEC decoder normally use a full address, data and control bus interface with the microprocessor.

A practical channel decoder

Figure 9.8 overleaf shows the circuit diagram for a Pace satellite channel decoder. The tuner (not shown) is a self-contained isolated unit which receives the modulated signals from the LNB, downconverts the carrier to a second IF and produces two analogue signals: in-phase (I) and quadrature (Q). These two signals are fed into pins 12 and 16 (AIN-I and AIN-Q) of the dual ADC U100, which converts them into two 6-bit digital signals (DI1–QI5 and DQ1–DQ5). The sampling rate is set by a control signal from the QPSK demodulator to pin 21 (VCOINP) which controls an in-built VCO. The sampling rate is set to twice the symbol (i.e. phase) or baud rate. If the baud rate is high, the sampling rate is set to twice the baud rate; if the baud rate is low, the sampling rate is set to three

Fig. 9.8 *Part of a Pace channel decoder*

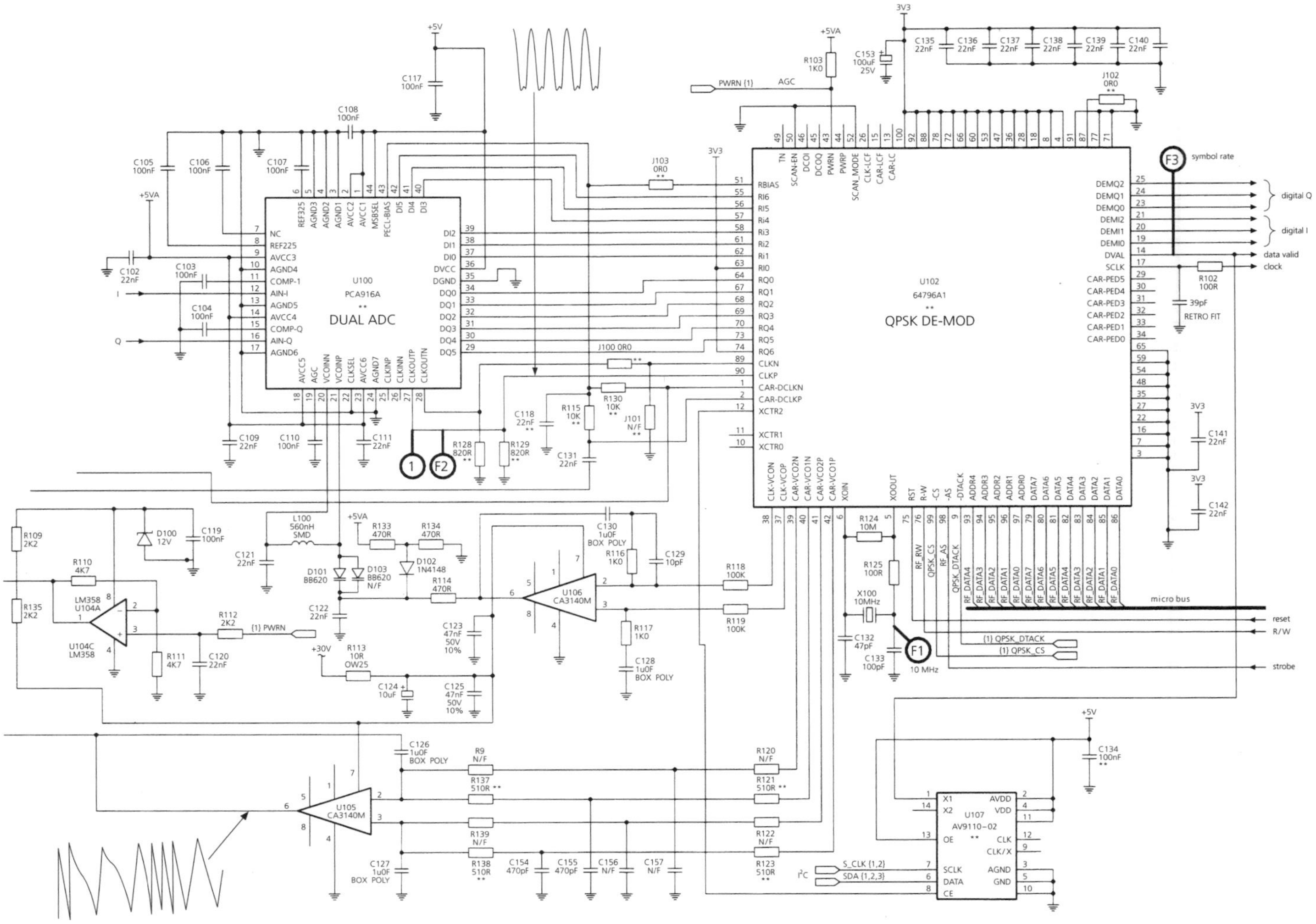

times the baud rate. The I and Q outputs from the dual ADC (pins 29–34 and 37–42) are fed into the QPSK demodulator U102. The demodulator receives the I and Q samples at pins 55–62 (RI6–RI1) and pins 74–67 (RQ6–RQ1). Bits RI0 and RQ0 are tied high at 3.3 V. The demodulator converts the digitized I and Q signals into a bitstream, itself sampled at twice the baud rate and quantized into 3-bit codes. The I and Q bitstreams are thus represented by a 3-bit coded digital signal which appears at the output on pins 19, 20 and 21 (DEMI0–DEMI2) and pins 23, 24 and 25 (DEMQ0–DEMQ2).

Tuner local oscillator control is carried out by carrier synchronization pins 39–42 (CAR-VCO2N, CAR-VCO1N, CAR-VCO2P and CAR-VCO1P), which send the appropriate signal to the tuner via op-amp U105. AGC is provided by PWRN signal at pin 43, which is fed to the tuner via integrating op-amp U104A. The ADC sampling rate is set by signals at pins 37 and 38 (CLK-VCOP and CLK-VCON), which are fed to op-amp U104B before going into pin 21 of the dual ADC chip. Reference frequency 100 MHz × 100 at pins 5 and 6 is used to synchronize and control the sampling rate of the ADC and the local oscillator at the tuner. Interfacing with the system microcontroller is carried out by an 8-bit data bus (DATA0–DATA7 on pins 79 to 86), a 5-bit address bus (ADDR0–ADDR4 on pins 93 to 97) and control lines: read/write (RF_RW on pin 76), chip select (QPSK_CS on pin 99) and data acknowledge (QPSK_DTACK on pin 9). The five address lines ADDR0–ADDR4 are multiplexed with the first five data lines DATA0–DATA4 on the microcomputer chip. For this reason, an address strobe control line RF_AS (pin 98) is used to latch the address lines into the demodulator.

Terrestrial front end

The main components of a DTTV front end are shown in Fig. 9.9. The tuner receives UHF-modulated signals from the terrestrial aerial, selects the appropriate channel and produces a modulated VHF intermediate frequency (IF). Before the intermediate frequency can be processed, it is fed into a downconverter to produce what is known as a low IF. The downconverter removes the VHF carrier and retains the baseband signals with a centre frequency of 4.75 MHz or thereabouts, depending on the chipset used.

Fig. 9.9 *DTV terrestrial front end*

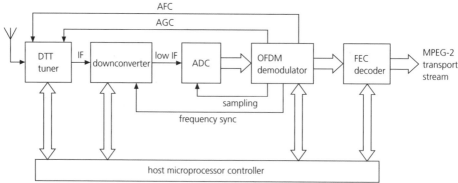

The low IF is digitized by an ADC using a sampling frequency derived from the OFDM demodulator. This is followed by the OFDM demodulator itself, which retrieves the original modulating transport stream for transmission to the FEC decoder. All units are fully controllable by the host system microprocessor.

Downconverter

A downconverter consists of a mixer followed by a lowpass filter (Fig. 9.10). The standard function of a mixer is to change the frequency of an input signal. This is carried out by 'mixing' the original signal (frequency f_1) and a separate signal (frequency f_0) obtained from a local oscillator. The two signals are multiplied by the mixer to produce two beat frequencies: the sum $(f_1 + f_0)$ and the difference $(f_1 - f_0)$.

Fig. 9.10 *Downconverter*

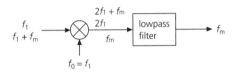

If the local oscillator frequency equals the input frequency $(f_1 = f_0)$ then $f_1 - f_0$ will cancel out, leaving only $f_1 + f_0 = 2f_1$.

Given that input 1 is $\cos \omega_1 t$ and input 2 is $\cos \omega_0 t$, where $\omega_1 = 2\pi f_1$ and $\omega_0 = 2\pi f_0$. Then

$$\cos \omega_1 t \cos \omega_0 t = \tfrac{1}{2} \cos(\omega_1 t + \omega_0 t) + \tfrac{1}{2} \cos(\omega_1 t - \omega_0 t)$$

If $f_1 = f_0$ then

$$\cos \omega_1 t \cos \omega_0 t = \tfrac{1}{2} \cos 2\omega_1 t$$

If the input signal contains a side frequency $f_1 + f_m$ as well as f_1 then the output will contain the following beat frequencies:

$$(f_1 + f_m) + f_1 = 2f_1 + f_m$$
$$f_1 + f_1 = 2f_1$$
$$(f_1 + f_m) - f_1 = f_m$$
$$f_1 - f_1 = 0$$

If the cut-off frequency of the lowpass filter is arranged to remove $2f_1$, the output will contain the modulating frequency f_m only.

In the case of terrestrial DTV, the side frequencies represent the sum of the OFDM 16-QAM or 64-QAM carriers, hence the waveform in Fig. 9.11.

Fig. 9.11 *Typical low IF waveform*

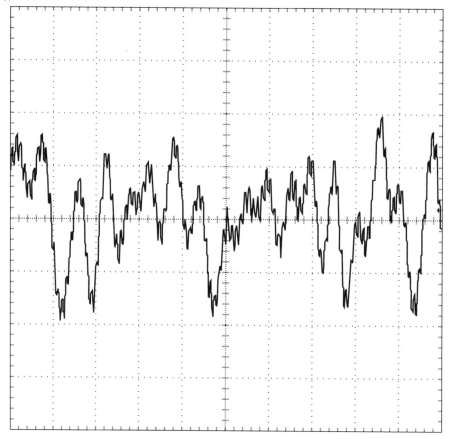

Figure 9.12 shows the circuit diagram for a tuner followed by a downconverter used in a Pace terrestrial decoder. The UHF signal from the aerial goes through two amplifying stages, RF Amp1 and RF Amp 2. Both amplifiers use high frequency FET transistors. The output from RF Amp1 is fed to a buffer (common collector) amplifier which routes the RF signal back out of the set-top box. This signal is then available for analogue television receivers or VCR machines. Following RF amplification, the signal is fed to the tuner. The tuner is controlled by an I²C bus (pins 4 and 5) The input is fed into pin 1, AGC into pin 2 and a balanced output at an IF of 36.25 MHz (IF1 and IF2) is available at pins 11 and 10. The two IFs go through tuned circuit X100 (tuned to 36.25 MHz) before the IF amplifying stage, which consists of a buffer (common collector) amplifier TR2 and a common emitter amplifier TR3. The output goes through a second tuned circuit on its way to the downconverter TUA6190x (U100). The two IFs enter the downconverter at pins 5 and 6 with balanced low IF (baseband) outputs OUT1 and OUT2 available at pins 10 and 9. OUT1 is terminated with a 10 kΩ resistor R114 and the other output is fed to an emitter follower buffer TR4 for further processing. A 40.739 MHz crystal provides stable local oscillator frequency. IF automatic gain control signal is provided at pin 8.

Fig. 9.12 Pace's tuner/downconverter stage

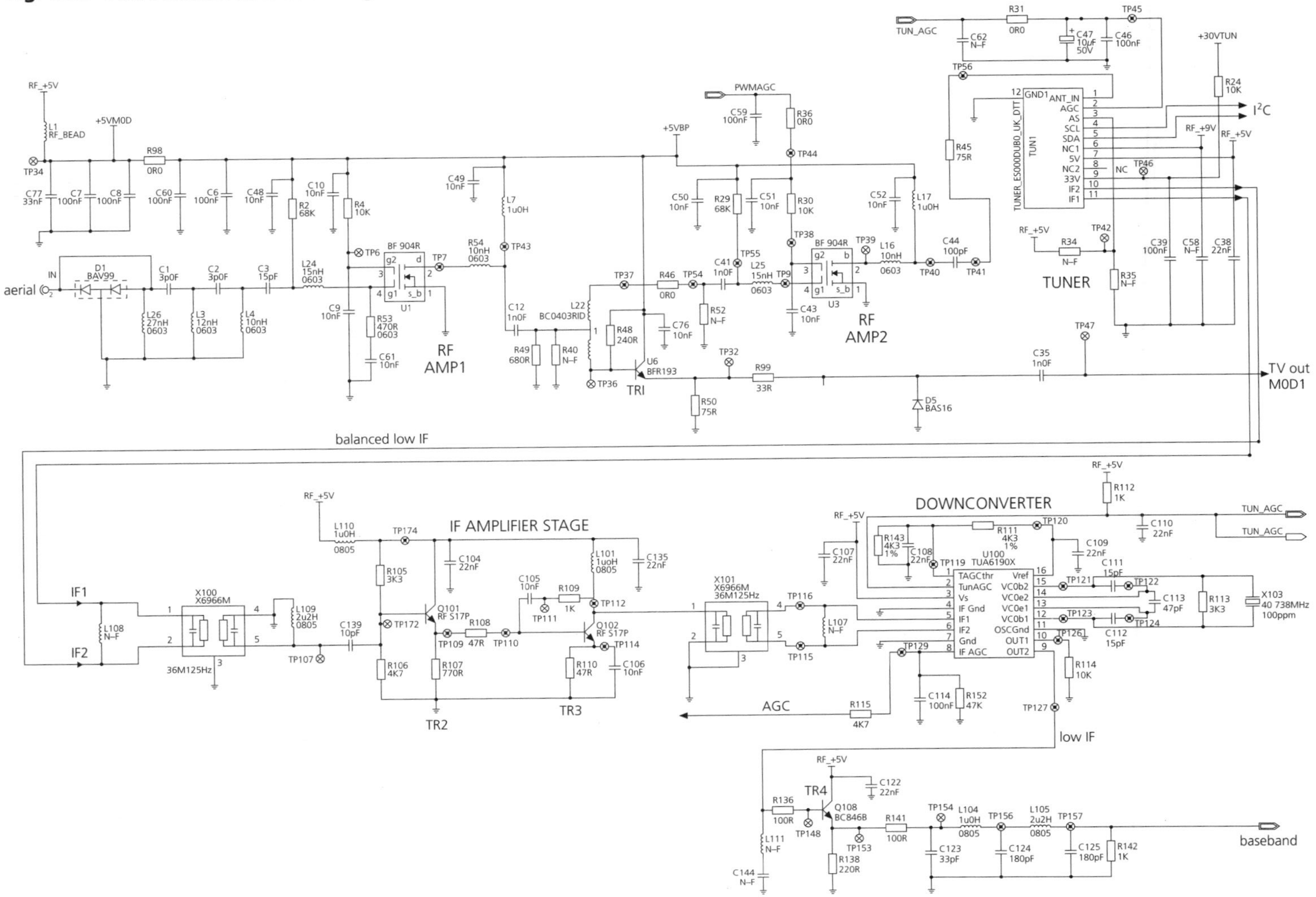

Fig. 9.13 *OFDM demodulator*

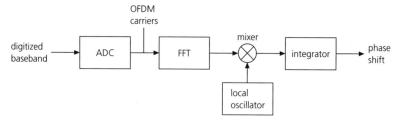

OFDM demodulator

The purpose of the demodulator is to retrieve data bitstream, which is represented by the phase shift of the carriers. The basic principles of the OFDM demodulator are illustrated in Fig. 9.13.

The input to the demodulator is the continuous waveform which was constructed by a DAC from the individually phase-modulated OFDM carriers at the transmitting stage. The first step is therefore to deconstruct the signal into its original frequency components, i.e. the original OFDM carriers. This is achieved by an FFT processor. As the FFT processor is a digital device, the input is digitized by an ADC before it is fed into the FFT processor (Fig. 9.14). The sampling frequency for the ADC is derived from the demodulator itself. The modulated OFDM carriers are then fed into the mixer.

The mixer is fed with two signals: an OFDM carrier and local oscillator signal of equal frequency, f_c. If the OFDM carrier contains no phase shift, an output signal with a beat frequency of $2f_c$ will be obtained. However, if the OFDM carrier is phase modulated, the phase angle will be produced at the output together with the $2f_c$ beat signal.

Suppose that input 1 = cos $\omega_c t + \theta$ and input 2 = cos $\omega_c t$, where $\omega_c = 2\pi f_c$. Then

$$\cos(\omega_c t + \theta)\cos \omega_c t = \tfrac{1}{2}\cos(\omega_c t + \theta + \omega_c t) + \tfrac{1}{2}\cos(\omega_c t + \theta - \omega_c t)$$

$$= \tfrac{1}{2}\cos(2\omega_c t + \theta) + \tfrac{1}{2}\cos \theta$$

The phase angle may be separated and extracted using a filter. While this is possible for a few carriers, it is not practical for several thousand, as is the case with the OFDM technique. The process is further complicated by the fact that each local oscillator frequency will beat with all the other OFDM carrier frequencies, producing millions of beat frequencies of differences and sums. A technique has to be devised to remove all beat signals and leave only the phase shift angles. This is where the integrator comes in.

Integrator

This technique is based on the fact that the integral of a sine wave over one complete cycle is zero. This is because integrating a waveform over a period of time is a method of calculating the area under the curve, along the zero line over that period of time. Figure 9.14a shows that the area of a sine wave over a period of one cycle is zero. The

Fig. 9.14 *Zero: the integral of a sine wave over a complete cycle*

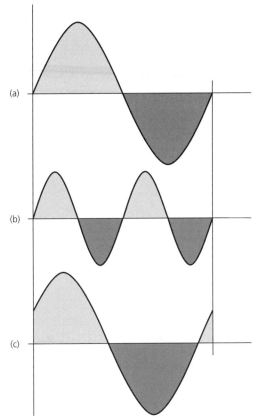

same result is obtained if the frequency is doubled (Fig. 9.14b) or trebled, etc., or if it experiences a phase shift (Fig. 9.14c).

Remember that a precise frequency spacing separated the OFDM carriers. In the 2K mode, the carrier spacing is 4464 Hz. Every OFDM carrier is therefore a multiple of 4464. Thus if the signals from the downconverter are integrated over the periodic time of one cycle of the carrier spacing, namely 1/4464 = 224 μs, all carriers will be beaten to zero. The only element left will be the phase shift of each carrier, which represents the transmitted data bits. The process is then repeated for every symbol to extract the next part of the bitstream, and so on.

A practical channel decoder

Figure 9.15 shows a circuit diagram for a Pace OFDM demodulator and FEC decoding stage using L64780 and L64724. The baseband signal from the downconverter enters the OFDM demodulator at pin 157 with the output at pins 51–53 and 56–58. The OFDM demodulator is controlled by the I²C serial bus at pins 118 and 129 with hex address FE. The FEC processor receives the input at pins 30–32 and 20, 23 and 24 with VALID

Fig. 9.15 Pace's channel decoder

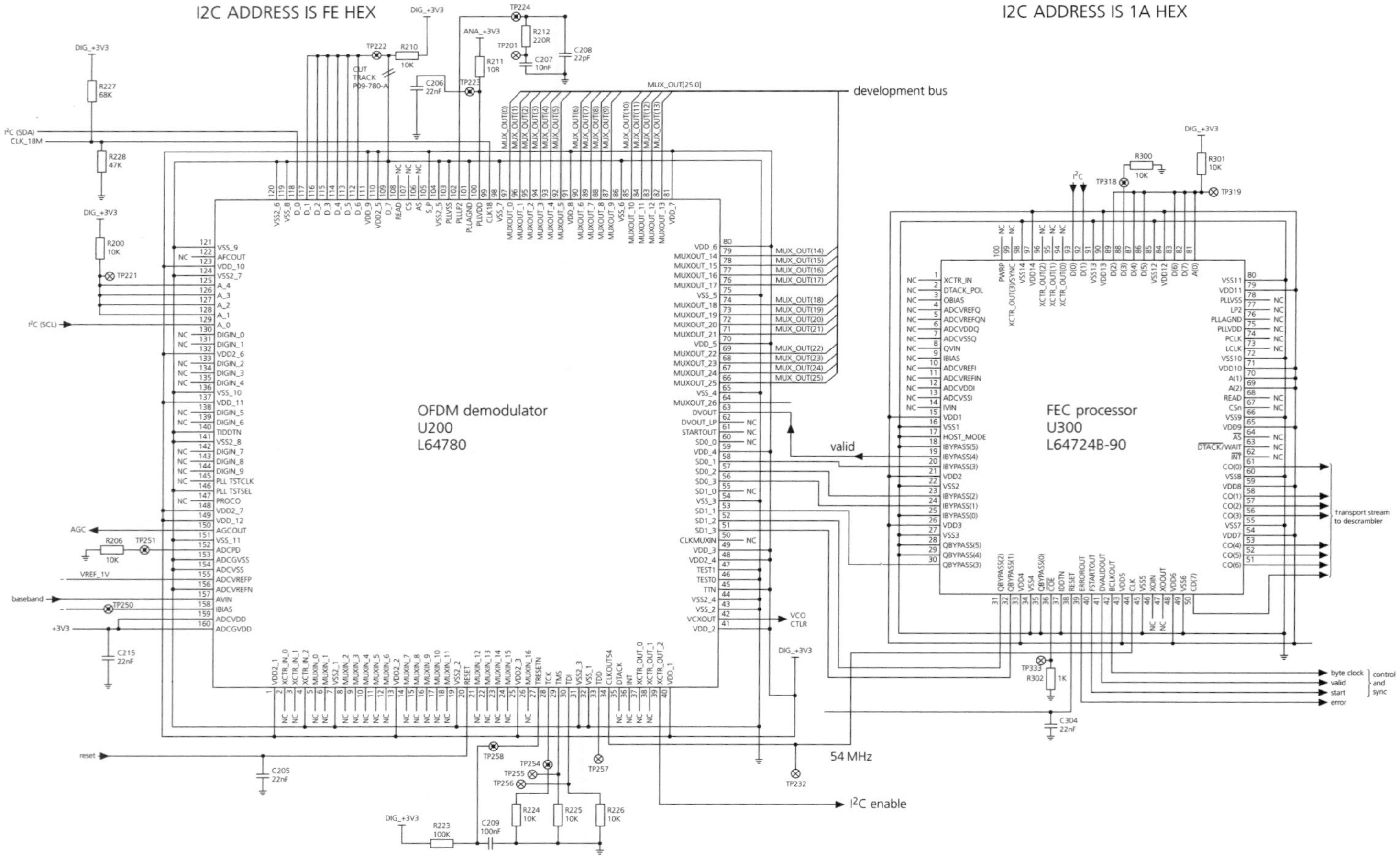

Fig. 9.16 *Single-chip channel decoder*

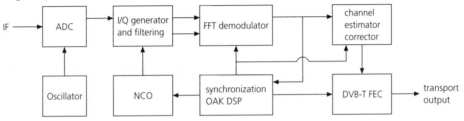

control at pin 19. The FEC chip is also I²C controlled at pins 92 and 93 with a hex address of 1A. The transport stream appears in the form of an 8-bit word at pins 50–53, 56–58 and 61. Transport packets that cannot be corrected by the FEC are indicated by the error signal at pin 38.

Single-chip demodulator and FEC decoder

Further integration has reduced the chip count by incorporating the OFDM demodulator and the FEC decoder in a single chip. An example of this is the VLSI Technology VES9600 single-chip channel decoder (Fig. 9.16). The VES9600 is a system-on-a-chip (SOC) device with an OAK processor core. It incorporates an ADC, OFDM demodulator and FEC decoder. It supports both 2K and 8K FFT, QPSK, 16-QAM and 64-QAM, Viterbi decoder, convolutional deinterleaving, Reed–Solomon decoding and guard intervals of 1/32, 1/16, 1/8 and 1/4. The input comes directly from a downconverter and the output is a transport stream packet suitable for feeding directly into a demultiplexer.

Chipset for satellite front end

The number of chips needed to build a satellite DTV front end depends on the choice of chipset. Invariably, the QPSK demodulator and the FEC decoder are integrated on a single chip such as the L64796 and the L64704 used by Pace decoders.

A single-chip DTV satellite (DTVS) front end, sometimes called a channel receiver, is also available, e.g. VLSI Technology's VES1893 (Fig. 9.17). The *I* and *Q* input signals come directly from the tuner, and the output transport stream packets are suitable for feeding into a transport demultiplexer. Fully programmable by I²C bus, the chip features a QPSK demodulator, FEC decoder, dual ADC and programmable anti-aliasing filters.

Fig. 9.17 *Block diagram of VES1893 single-chip satellite front end*

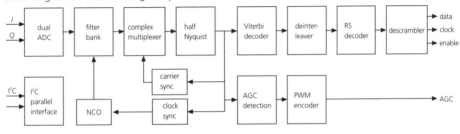

Fig. 9.18 *LSI DTTV front-end chipset*

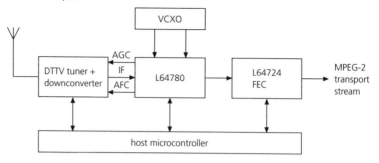

The ADC may be bypassed, allowing for direct interface with I and Q digitized baseband signals. There is in-built carrier recovery and clock synchronization using an internal numerically controlled oscillator (NCO). AGC is provided by a phase width modulation (PWM) encoder.

Chipset for terrestrial front end

The number of chips actually used by manufacturers depends on the level of integration of the chipset. LSI Logic, in cooperation with the BBC, designed the L64780 OFDM demodulator chip, which incorporates an ADC together with an OFDM demodulator.

Figure 9.18 shows the complete LSI chipset for a terrestrial front end consisting of

- Digital terrestrial tuner and downconverter
- L64780 OFDM demodulator
- L64724 FEC decoder

The basic architecture of the L64780 OFDM demodulator chip is shown in Fig. 9.19. The input to the device is a low IF analogue COFDM signal with a centre frequency of 4.75 MHz. The first operation performed by the chip is to sample the input signal at a rate equal to 4 × centre frequency (4 × 4.75 = 18.29 MHz). The next stage is a real-to-complex converter. This block takes the 'real' input signal centred on 4.75 MHz and produces a complex signal centred on zero frequency (0 Hz). The complex signal is then fed in parallel to the timing/synchronization block and the FFT processing block. The timing/synchronization block uses the complex signal to derive a signal that is used to control the external voltage-controlled oscillator (VCXO).

The FFT block has four modes of operation. It is able to perform a 2K or an 8K point transform. Secondly, it can perform the transform in either direction. FFT is used for a DTTV receiver front end. However, the same chip can be used in applications requiring OFDM modulation, and here inverse FFT is employed. Frequency synchronization is carried out immediately after the FFT block. This section provides an output signal that adjusts the frequency of the downconverter as well as an automatic frequency control (AFC) control signal for the tuner. The FFT demodulator generates the I and Q signals for each carrier, demodulates them and reproduces the original modulating symbol. The output of the FFT demodulator is therefore the original stream of bits used to modulate the OFDM carriers at the transmitting end. Processing these signals involves phase error

Fig. 9.19 *OFDM demodulator: L64780 architecture*

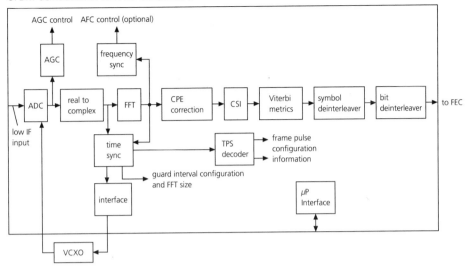

correction and deinterleaving. Correction involves common phase error (CPE) correction, and Viterbi decoding using channel state information (CSI) data. Deinterleaving involves symbol and bit interleaving in that order. The data from the convolutional deinterleaver is then passed off chip to the FEC decoder.

Conditional access

Conditional access (CA) is the process of determining which individual user will be able to receive broadcast services. It is an essential part of the business of commercial subscription and pay TV. It is also used where the programmes being broadcast are for specific geographical areas or for controlled audiences such as horse racing services for betting shops. Services with conditional access specification are scrambled by the broadcaster in accordance with a standard algorithm. Access control is achieved by including unscrambled control data within the transport stream or PES packets. At the receiving end, the service is descrambled only if the user has an entitlement to access that service. The scrambling used in the context of conditional access must be distinguished from the pseudo-random scrambling used for energy dispersal.

The CA system thus consists of two parts: scrambling/descrambling and access control. Of these two parts, only the scrambling and descrambling techniques have been standardized. Access control methods are proprietary, i.e. they are determined by the broadcaster. Thus, at any one time, a number of CA systems may be in use in the marketplace. Figure 9.20 shows the basic components of a conditional access descrambler unit. It consists of two main parts: a conditional access interface and a conditional access module (CAM). The CA interface is a common interface with standard digital video broadcasting (DVB) specification. It connects the proprietary CAM to the host decoder system. It carries the whole transport stream to and from the CAM. The CAM, which

Fig. 9.20 *Conditional access*

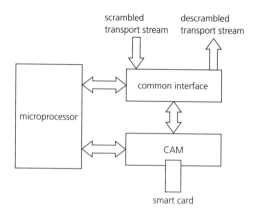

scrambled   descrambled
transport stream   transport stream

common interface

microprocessor

CAM

smart card

may be a self-contained detachable unit, provides conditional access and descrambling facilities. It selects the services from the transport stream, descrambles them and returns them back to the transport demultiplexer via the interface. Transport packets are selected by the descrambler within the CAM using their packet identification (PID) numbers supplied by the host microprocessor. The descrambler examines the scrambling control bits in the packet header to ascertain whether the selected services are scrambled or not. If they are not scrambled, the transport stream is returned back to the transport demultiplexer for further processing. If the packets are scrambled, the descrambler examines the CA control data to determine whether the user has rights to access the selected services. If the user has the appropriate rights to access the services, the packets are descrambled. For descrambling to take place, conditional access data has to be extracted from the transport stream and passed to the smart card. The CA data, which includes *entitlement control messages (ECMs)* and *entitlement management messages (EMMs)*, is fed into the smart card. The smart card decodes these messages and returns decoded control words to the descrambler to enable the process to be synchronized.

Because the CA interface allows the module to extract selected data from the transport stream multiplexer and deliver it to the host decoder, it can be used to support a number of other applications such as an *electronic programme guide (EPG)* and *parental control*. In general, the CA interface allows new features to be introduced and delivered to the host decoder without requiring the host to understand them beforehand. It also allows the security system to be upgraded as it becomes necessary.

By using a standard scrambling system within the MPEG bitstream, it is possible for the DTV transmission to carry multiple control messages for the scrambled broadcast. These control messages may be generated by a number of different CA systems. This technique is known as *Simulcrypt*. Simulcrypt provides a facility to deliver one programme to a number of different decoders with different CA control systems. Conversely, it allows for transition from one CA control system to another for any given type of decoder. This latter facility provides a cheap and simple way for a broadcaster to change the CA control system if the scrambling code is cracked by pirates.

10 MPEG decoding

Before the video and audio decoding stage, the transport stream must go through a demultiplexing process to select the video and audio PES packets of the selected programme and any other related services. This process is carried out by the *transport demultiplexer (demux)*.

The transport demux

The input to the demux (Fig. 10.1) is an 8-bit wide transport stream consisting of video, audio or other service information belonging to four, five or more different programmes organized into 188-byte transport packets. The transport stream is examined to ascertain if CA scrambling is employed. If it is not, the CAM is bypassed and the transport stream is processed in the normal way. If the programme is scrambled, the CAM ascertains whether

Fig. 10.1 *Transport demultiplexer*

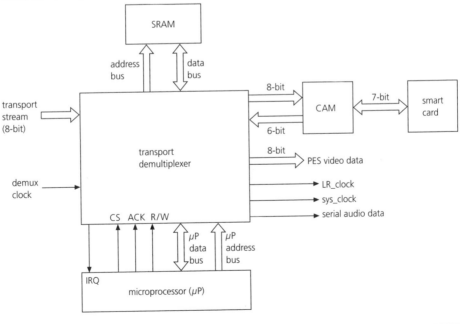

Fig. 10.2 *Pace circuit for a transport demultiplexer*

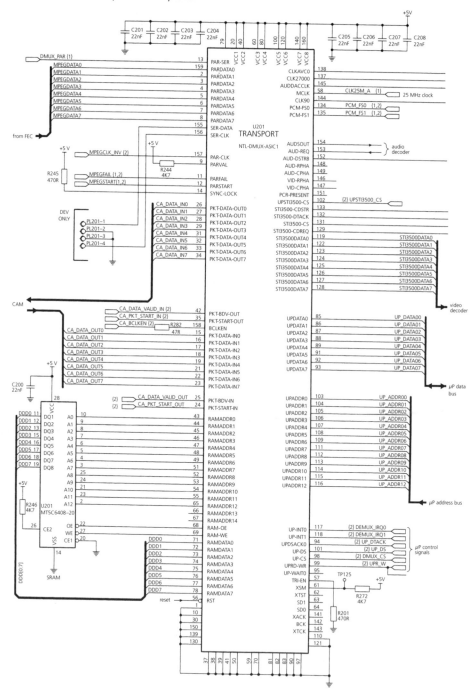

the user has access rights to the programme. If so, the transport stream is descrambled and returned to the demux for further processing. If the user has no entitlement to view the programme, the transport stream is blocked, giving a blank display on the television screen. A message may be displayed to inform the user of the problem.

The central task of the demux is to extract the transport packets that belong to the selected programme. To do this, the demux first extracts the packet with PID zero. This contains the programme association table (PAT) in which the demux will find the PID of the packet that contains the programme map table (PMT). Once the PMT is opened, the demux is able to identify the relevant PID for all the components of the particular programme and proceed to extract them from the transport stream. The 188-byte transport packets are then reconstructed to obtain their original elementary stream packets: video, audio and service PESs. The video PES packets are sent to the video decoder along an 8-bit wide video data bus. In the case of the audio PES packets, the demultiplexer converts them into a serial format and sends them out to the audio decoder with a number of audio control signals, including system_clock and LR_clock, which ensure synchronization and stereophonic reproduction.

Fast static memory SRAM (access time 15–20 μs) is used to store selected video, audio and other service packets for later release in bursts. Dedicated address and data buses are provided for that purpose. The transport demux is interfaced to the main microprocessor via a data bus and an address bus together with a number of control lines: read/write (R/W), acknowledge (ACK) and chip select (CS) as well as an interrupt request (IRQ) line.

This whole process is performed under the control of the host microprocessor. The demultiplexer operates on its own system clock, typically 25 MHz (as distinguished from the 27 MHz PCR for the data stream).

A demux chip

Figure 10.2 shows a typical transport demux chip together with a 20 μs SRAM buffer chip MT5C6408–20 (the speed in microseconds of the memory chip is indicated by the number immediately to the right of the dash). The 8-bit wide transport stream (PARDATA 0–7) enters the demux chip at pin 159 and pins 2–8. Three control signals are used to control the transport stream (Fig. 10.3):

- PARSTART (pin 12) goes high for the first byte of each data packet of the transport stream
- PARFAIL (pin 11) goes low if the data received has errors which have not been corrected by the FEC
- Data clock PAR-CLK (pin 157)

A register in the demux determines whether the received data needs to be passed to the conditional access module. If so, the received data is clocked into the conditional access module on pins 26–34 and arrives back on pins 15–23. Once again, three control signals are employed:

- CA_PKT_START_IN on pin 35 goes high to indicate the first byte of each data packet in the transport stream
- CA_DATA_VALID_IN on pin 42 goes high if the data received from the FEC has no errors in it
- CA_BCLKEN on pin 158 for clock synchronization

Fig. 10.3 *Three signals control the transport stream: PARSTART, PARFAIL, PAR-CLK*

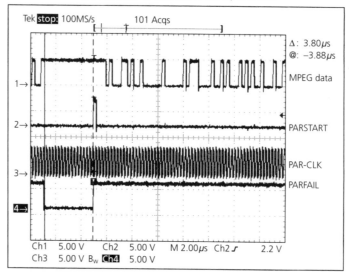

The demux filters off the video data and sends it to the video decoder along an 8-bit wide bus (ST13500DATA) on pin 119 and pins 122–128. Access to the SRAM chip is via an 8-bit data bus (RAMDATA0–RAMDATA7) on pins 71–78 and a 13-bit address bus (RAMDR0–RAMDR112) on pins 43–65 with Output Enable, i.e. Read Enable (RAM-OE) on pin 68 and write enable (RAM-WE) on pin 69.

Audio data is sent to the audio decoder serially on pin 154 (AUDSOUT) with a data strobe control line (AUD-DSTB) on pin 152. Data is clocked out on the falling edge of the clock and when it is received by the audio decoder, the audio decoder sends an AUD-REQ signal to demux pin 153.

The demux operates on a 25 MHz clock arriving at pin 58. The demux is programmed and controlled by the microprocessor via an 8-bit bus (UP_DATA on pins 85–93) and a 13-bit address bus (UP_ADDR on pins 103–109 and 111–116) together with four control signals:

- Read/write (UPR_W) pin 99
- Chip select (DMUX_CS) pin 98
- Data strobe (UP_DS) pin 101
- Data acknowledge (UP_DTACK) pin 94.

The demux has two interrupt request lines: DEMUX_IRQ1 (pin 117) and DEMUX_IRQ2 (pin 118).

SoC transport processor

The functions of the transport demux and the microprocessor may be combined to form a system-on-a-chip, normally called a transport processor. A typical pin-out is shown in Fig. 10.4. The input data consists of MPEG-2 transport packets together

Fig. 10.4 *Transport processor SoC: typical pin-out*

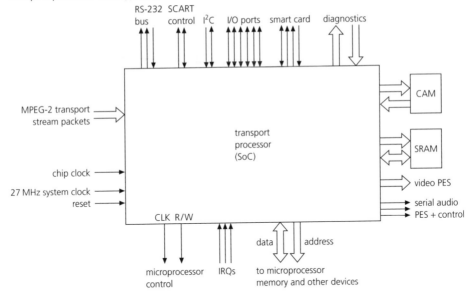

with the 27 MHz system clock. Demultiplexing is carried out under the control of the onboard microprocessor core, which also performs the necessary software and hardware control of other devices via the data and address buses or the I²C serial bus. The microprocessor core provides a number of I/O ports and an RS-232 interface. A diagnostic bus is normally provided which may be used to connect to measuring and diagnostic devices.

Video decoder

The function of the MPEG video decoder (Fig. 10.5) is to restore the picture to its original form. This involves data decompression, inverse DCT, reconstructing the picture from the I, P and B frames and reproducing the original luminance Y and chrominance C_R and C_B components of each frame. Reconstruction of the picture involves simultaneous storage of the transmitted frames, making the necessary comparisons to rebuild the complete frames. A large memory store is therefore necessary. The memory store required for storing the different frames is provided by a minimum 16 Mbits of DRAM memory store. In some receivers, the B frames are not utilized and the picture is rebuilt from the I and P frames only. This procedure requires smaller DRAM memory store and thus reduces the cost.

The picture having been reconstructed, the luminance Y and chrominance C_R and C_B pixel data is sent to the PAL encoder along an 8-bit multiplexed YC data bus. The PAL encoder produces a standard 625-line, 25 pictures per second television signal. The start of each scan-line is indicated by an *HSYNC* control signal. Odd and even (top or bottom) fields are indicated by two other control signals, *ODDE* and *EVEN*. The

Fig. 10.5 *Video decoder*

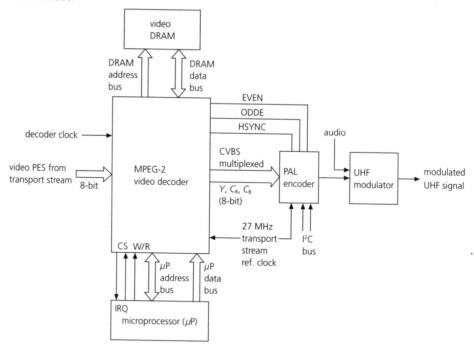

composite video (CVBS) signal is fed into a UHF modulator as shown in Fig. 10.4. Both the video decoder and the PAL encoder are clocked by the 27 MHz programme reference clock to synchronize the bit acquisition. The video decoder itself operates on its own clock of around 55 MHz.

The decoder is programmed and controlled by the microprocessor via an address and data bus together with a number of control signals, including R/W and CS. One IRQ is provided for the video decoder to request processing routines such as the start of a field. The PAL encoder is controlled by the I²C bus which sets the operational parameters of the encoder.

The MPEG video decoder usually carries out other functions, integrated for reasons of efficiency. Two such functions are aspect ratio conversion (from 16:9 to 4:5 format) and onscreen display (OSD). OSD is able to provide 16 or more colours in any defined rectangular region of the screen up to the maximum display resolution of 720 × 576. OSD information may be overlaid on the picture information by making some pixels transparent through assigning a specific colour defined as transparent so that the picture information appears through the OSD.

A decoder chip

A typical video decoder chip is shown in Fig. 10.6. The 8-bit wide video data (ST1500DATA) from the transport demux is received on pins 103–110. The microprocessor accesses the decoder via the same video data bus (ST1500DATA) and a 6-bit address

Fig. 10.6 Pace circuit for a video decoder

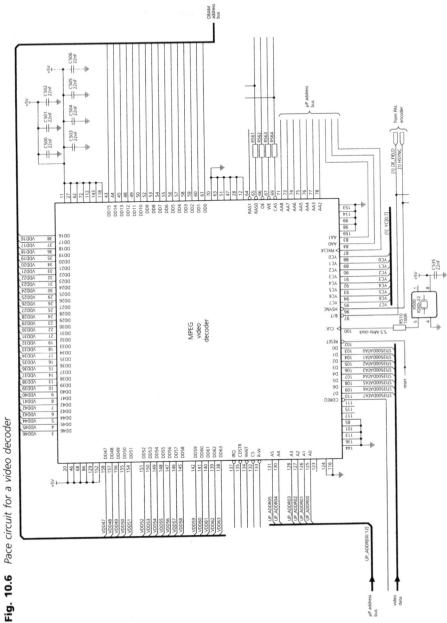

bus (UP_ADDR), pins 125–128 and 130 and 131. It allows the microprocessor to select one of $6^2 = 64$ registers inside the video decoder. Data inside these registers sets the parameters to be used in the decoding process. The 16 Mbit video DRAM is accessed via a 64-bit data bus (DD0–DD63) and an 8-bit address bus (AA0–AA7). The output to the PAL encoder is carried along an 8-bit bus (YC0–YC7), pins 88–95, which carries multiplexed pixel data Y, C_R and C_B. Synchronization between the video decoder and the PAL encoder is obtained by a common pixel 27 MHz clock (PIXCLK on pin 87), horizontal sync (HSYNC on pin 96) and vertical sync called bottom/top (B/T on pin 97). The decoder operates on a 55 MHz clock generated by a crystal oscillator and fed into pin 100.

Audio decoder

The audio decoder (Fig. 10.7) is a digital signal processing (DSP) chip which receives serial coded audio data together with audio control signals from the transport demux and carries out the necessary decoding to produce two serial pulse code modulation (PCM) left and right audio channels. The audio decoder can give an audio output at three different sampling rates: 32, 44.1 and 48 kHz. Information on the actual sampling rate used by the transmitter is provided by the transport demux, which extracts the information from the incoming transport stream. Audio buffering is provided by the DRAM store, which also provides the necessary 1 s delay. The decoder is fully programmed and controlled

Fig. 10.7 *Audio decoder*

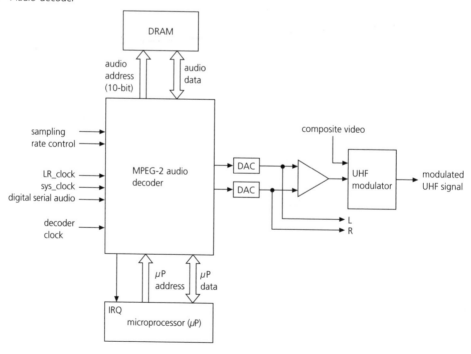

by the microprocessor with address bus and data buses and control lines R/W and CS. An interrupt request is provided in order for the decoder to inform the microprocessor of the occurrence of certain events and requesting services.

A decoder chip

A typical MPEG audio decoder chip is shown in Fig. 10.8. When the audio decoder is ready to receive data, it sends a request REQ signal to demux on pin 99. Digitally modulated serial data (SIN) is then sent to the decoder pin 88 together with a data strobe (DSTRB) on pin 93. The sampling rate is indicated by the logic states of signals FS0 and FS1 at pins 22 and 23 (Table 10.1).

The audio output to the audio DACs is PCMDATA on pin 20. The sampling clock labelled SCK (pin 19) for the DACs is produced by dividing the PCM clock (PCMCLK pin 14). The signal on pin 17 (LRCLK) indicates whether the data is left or right channel

Fig. 10.8 *Pace circuit for an audio decoder*

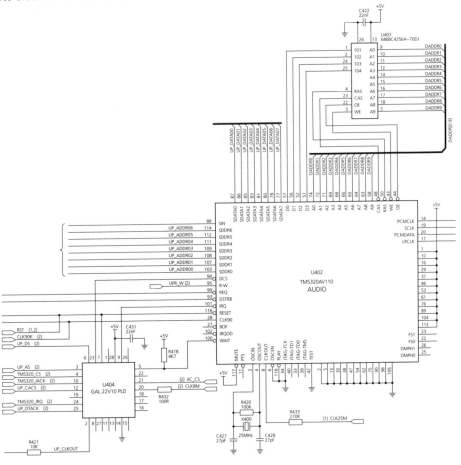

Table 10.1 *Decoder sampling rate is indicated by FS0 and FS1*		
FS0	*FS1*	*Sampling rate (kHz)*
0	0	44.1
0	1	32
1	0	48

Fig. 10.9 *The signal on pin 17 indicates whether the data is left or right channel*

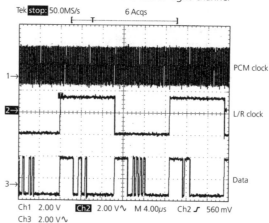

(Fig. 10.9). The interface to the microprocessor comprises an 8-bit data bus (and a 7-bit address bus which allows the microprocessor access to the decoder's registers). Read/write (R/W pin 95) is connected directly to the processor. Other controls pass through a *programmable logic device* (PLD) which translates these signals into a format that may be understood by the decoder. Apart from the 25 MHz sync lock (pin 8), the decoder also receives a 90 kHz clock from the transport demux on pin 28. This is used with a counter within the audio decoder to prevent false locking of the onboard clock to the transmitted clock. The memory chip provides the required 1 s delay to ensure audio and video synchronization. It uses DRAM with 70 ns access time and standard control lines RAS, CAS, OE and WE.

The SCART connection

SCART socket

Modern TV receivers are designed to receive direct audio/video (AV) input from external sources such as video recorders, camcorders, satellite receivers and digital television decoders. They also provide direct AV signals to peripherals such as video recorders and

Fig. 10.10 *SCART socket pin-out*

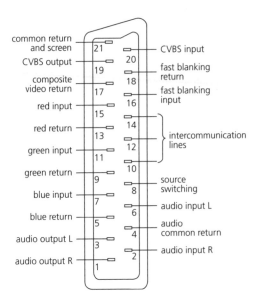

audio systems. The standard outlet for such facilities is the SCART socket connection (Fig. 10.10). The SCART connector allows direct RGB connection to a TV receiver as well as bidirectional composite video known as CVBS (composite video, blanking and sync) together with independent stereo sound channel connections. Table 10.2 lists the function of each pin and the expected type of signal it carries. Notice that while two types of video input (composite video pin 20 and RGB pins 15, 11 and 7) may be processed by the receiver, only composite video pin 19 is available as an output signal for external devices. Pins 10 and 12 are provided for intercommunication between devices connected to the SCART socket.

The SCART connector is a 21-pin non-reversible device. There are 20 pins available for connection; pin 21 is connected to the skirt and hence the chassis to provide the overall screening for cable communication.

SCART cable

When connecting two devices using a SCART cable, take care to ensure that the pins carrying output signals of one device are connected to the respective input pins of the second device and vice versa. The normal SCART cable has a male plug at either end to connect two devices, such as a DTV decoder and a TV receiver or VCR, via their respective SCART sockets. The crossover connections for such a plug-to-plug SCART cable are shown in Fig. 10.11. The cable consists of five sections:

- The audio section contains two independent input and output stereo channels. Screening for the four audio wires is provided by the audio earth connection at pin 4.

Table 10.2 *SCART socket pins and their function*

Pin	Function specification	Signal
1	Right channel audio out	0.5 V into 1 kΩ
2	Right channel audio in	0.5 V into 10 kΩ
3	Left channel audio out	0.5 V into 1 kΩ
4	Audio earth	
5	Blue earth	
6	Left channel audio in	0.5 V into 10 kΩ
7	Blue in	0.7 V into 75 Ω
8	Source switching (9–12 V)	not specific but usually max 12 V into 10 kΩ
9	Green earth	
10	Intercommunication line	
11	Green in	0.7 V into 75 Ω
12	Intercommunication line	
13	Red earth	
14	Intercommunication line earth	
15	Red in	0.7 V into 75 Ω
16	Fast RGB blanking	varies (1–3 V)
17	CVBS earth	
18	Fast blanking earth	
19	CVBS out	1 V into 75 Ω
20	CVBS in	1 V into 75 Ω
21	Socket earth	

Fig. 10.11 *Plug-to-plug SCART cable*

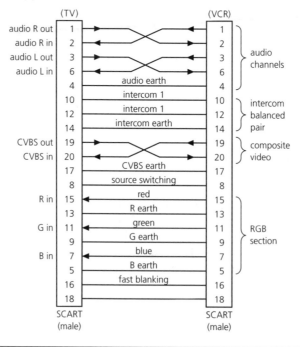

- The composite video section consists of two CVBS channels (input and output). A 75 Ω coax is used for each video channel, with the video earth providing the outer screen.
- The intercommunication data channels consist of two wires in a balanced pair arrangement with pin 14 providing the earth connection.
- Source or function switching consists of a single insulated wire connecting pin 8 at one end to pin 8 at the other end.
- The RGB section consists of three signal wires (RGB) and three wires for their respective earths together with a fast blanking.

SCART interface

Figure 10.12 shows a SCART connection between an IRD and a TV receiver. At the IRD side, the interface provides the switching, amplification and impedance matching necessary for routing the signals out of the decoder. Routing RGB signals to the TV receiver, the SCART interface will assert pin 8 (source switching) by applying a voltage of 9–12 V to the pin. Fast blanking is enabled at the receiver end. When this happens, the analogue RGB signals are blanked out and the incoming RGB signals are routed towards the appropriate drives for display on the screen.

Fig. 10.12 *SCART connection: STB to TV receiver*

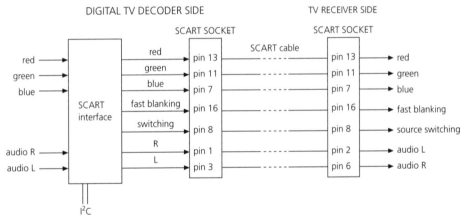

Dual-SCART receivers

Modern receivers provide two or more SCART sockets labelled TV, VCR, and so on. Where two sockets are provided, the connector marked TV provides RGB connection for a TV receiver. A SCART socket marked VCR (Fig. 10.13) would normally provide CVBS output (pin 19) connections together with audio L and R outputs (pins 3 and 1) for stereophonic sound. Also provided are input connections for CVBS (pin 20) and audio L and R input at pins 6 and 2 for routing composite video and stereophonic audio from one external source to another external source via the IRD.

Fig. 10.13 *SCART connection: STB to VCR*

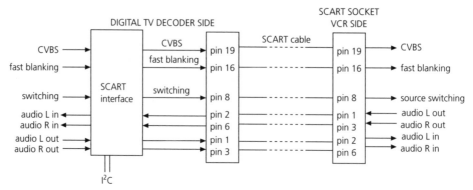

Video/audio decoder

Invariably, the functions of the video and audio decoders are combined in a single V/A processing chip (Fig. 10.14). Video and audio PES packets are fed into the V/A decoder together with the audio sampling rate and the 27 MHz system clock. The multiplexed Y, C_R and C_B video information is fed into a PAL encoder to produce a composite video, blanking and sync (CVBS) as well as RGB signals. The signals are fed into the appropriate SCART pins for direct transmission to a television receiver or VCR. The CVBS signal and a mono audio signal are used to modulate a UHF carrier which may be used to feed into the aerial socket of a TV receiver.

A PAL encoder chip

Figure 10.15 shows a typical PAL encoder. It receives the multiplexed luminance Y and chrominance C_R and C_B on an 8-bit bus YC0–YC7 (pins 36–43) and converts

Fig. 10.14 *Video/audio decoder*

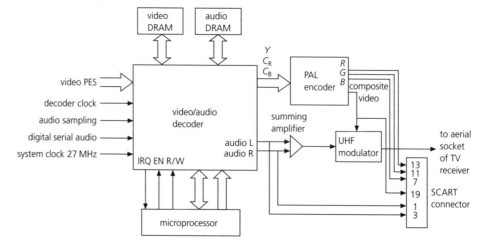

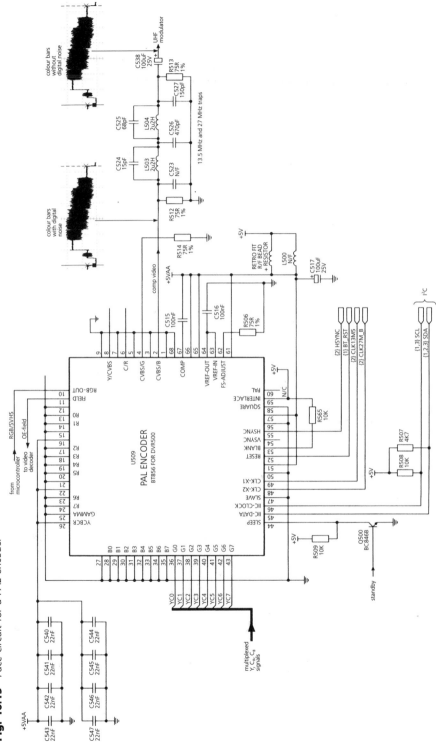

Fig. 10.15 Pace circuit for a PAL encoder

them into a standard PAL CVBS on pin 2. The encoder also provides RGB and SVHS outputs. The PAL encoder requires two locks, 25 MHz (pin 48) and 13.5 MHz (pin 49), which are obtained from the system clock generator. Control is carried out by the microcontroller via the I²C bus (pins 45 and 46). When the receiver is on standby, the microcontroller turns off transistor Q500 and puts the decoder in sleep mode (pin 44); this disables the encoder and produces a black screen. The composite video passes through a video reconstruction circuit comprising L503 and L504 and associated components. Digital noise is removed using a circuit with traps at 25 MHz and 13.5 MHz.

UHF modulator

The UHF modulator (Fig. 10.16) consists of a synthesized UHF modulator and a loop-through amplifier. The modulator has four components:

- An I²C-controlled phase-locked loop (PLL) frequency synthesizer
- An amplitude modulator
- An audio oscillator for the sound subcarrier
- A video clamp to ensure correct modulation index

Tuning of the modulator is carried out by a DC voltage (0–30 V) derived from the PLL frequency synthesizer. The audio signal is used to frequency modulate the sound subcarrier. The modulated sound carrier is then added to the clamped video signal and used to amplitude modulate a tuned UHF carrier. The modulated UHF is then fed into the loop-through amplifier, which mixes it with the signal from a second antenna.

When the digital decoder is on standby, the UHF synthesized oscillator is switched off by a command from the microcontroller via the I²C bus. But the loop-through amplifier operates normally so that the RF signal from a second antenna may loop through to the RF output socket.

Fig. 10.16 *UHF modulator*

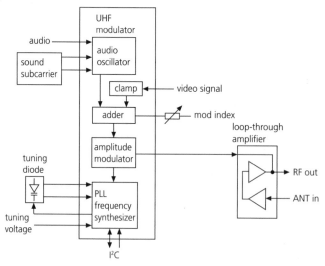

The single-chip set-top box

Advances in SoC technology and the use of high performance 64-bit CPUs have made it possible to combine the demodulating and decoding functions of a digital television IRD into a single chip (Fig. 10.17). The SoC chip carries out all the necessary processing and decoding for a satellite or cable decoder. Besides the SoC chip, all that is needed are a tuner, the conditional access module and some memory chips: ROM, DRAM and flash (for the onboard RISC microprocessor), SRAM (for transport multiplexing), video DRAM and audio DRAM.

Fig. 10.17 *Single-chip STB*

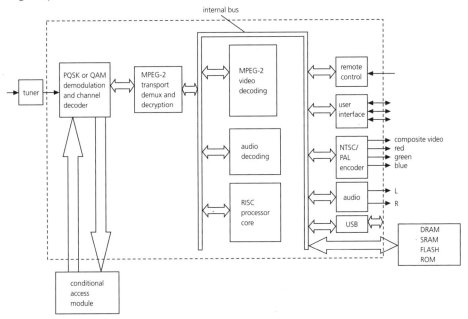

Satellite DTV receiver

Figure 10.18 shows a complete block diagram of a Pace satellite digital TV receiver. RF signals from the satellite dish are fed to the front end, which incorporates the tuner (TUN400), the dual ADC (U404) and QPSK demodulator/FEC processor (U403). The output, 188-byte scrambled transport packets (feclink), is fed into the conditional access unit (U1000 and associated chips) for descrambling (if appropriate) in order to reproduce the original MPEG transport stream (mpeglink). This is then fed into the SoC transport processor U300, which performs demultiplexing and uses the PID codes to extract the video, audio and other service PES packets belonging to the selected programme. The selected PES packets are then fed into the A/V decoder (U322) to produce video (ccir601) and audio (dig_audio_a) information. The video information is fed to a video

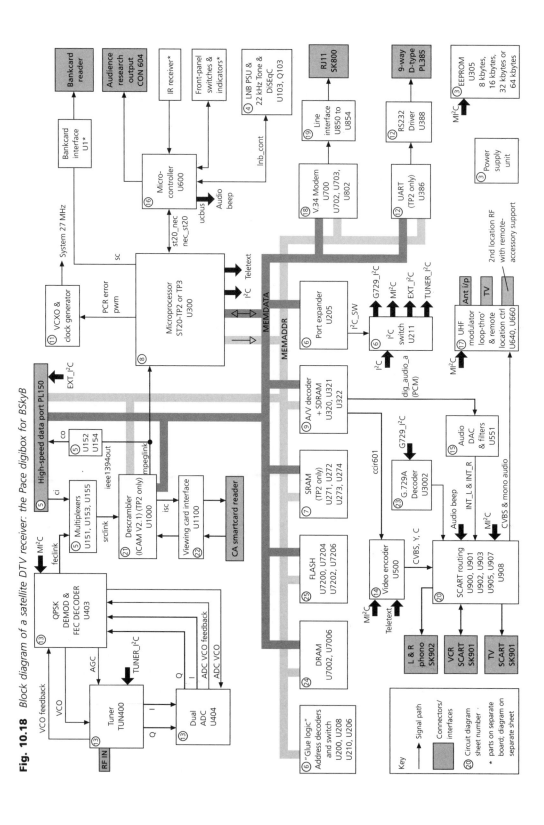

Fig. 10.18 *Block diagram of a satellite DTV receiver: the Pace digibox for BSkyB*

encoder (U500) to generate luminance and chrominance as well as CVBS signals for display on a television receiver via a SCART connector or UHF modulator (U640, U660). Furthermore, the demultiplexer also extracts the teletext packets and processes them for display.

Control is carried out by microprocessor U300 as well as microcontroller U600. The two chips communicate with each other via a two-line serial bus: st20_nec and nec_st20. The microprocessor controls the audio and video decoding including synchronization, the onboard transport stream demultiplexing process, the conditional access module, the high speed data port PL150, the modem and RS-232 interfaces; it also runs the receiver menu system. The microprocessor has its own clock, address (MEMADDR), data (MEMDATA), control bus structure and its own DRAM and flash memory stores. The non-volatile flash RAM chip is used to store software programs used in the decoding process. Software upgrades may be carried out off-air by first loading the new software into the DRAM chips and then transferring it to the non-volatile flash memory. The microprocessor provides further control via a direct I^2C serial bus and a switched I^2C (I^2C_SW) which controls the PAL or video encoder (U500), EEPROM, UHF modulator, QPSK demodulator/FEC processor, SCART routing, the high speed data port, the tuner and decoder U3002.

The U300 extracts the programme clock reference signals from the transport stream and feeds them into the clock generator to produce a synchronized 27 MHz system clock. The microcontroller monitors the power supply and decodes infrared information from the remote control handset and front panel buttons.

The IRD system supports a telephone connection via a modem (U700) together with the necessary line interface. It also supports RS-232 communication with UART (U386) and line driver (U388). The high speed data port provides a facility for MPEG transport stream packets to be available for other decoders.

Terrestrial DTV receiver

Figure 10.19 shows a complete block diagram of a Pace DTTV receiver. The difference between this and a satellite receiver is in the front end. RF signals from the terrestrial aerial are fed to the front end, which incorporates the tuner (TUN1), downconverter (U100), OFDM demodulator (U200) and FEC decoder (U300). The output, 188-byte scrambled transport packets (feclink) are fed into the transport processor TP4 (U200) via a 'multiplexer' (U154–156). The purpose of the multiplexer section is to allow the data to switch over to the PCMCIA port for external MPEG data transfer. TP4 is an SOC package which incorporates the conditional access unit. The transport processor performs the necessary demultiplexing and, using the PID codes, it extracts the video, audio and other service PES packets belonging to the selected programme.

The selected PES packets are then fed into the video/audio decoder (U300) to produce video and audio information. The video information is fed to a PAL encoder (U500) to generate luminance and chrominance as well as CVBS signals for display on a television receiver via a SCART connector or UHF modulator (U2). Furthermore, the demultiplexer also extracts the teletext packets and processes them for display. Control is carried out by microprocessor SOC U200 as well as NEC microcontroller U600.

Fig. 10.19 *Block diagram for Pace's DTTV receiver*

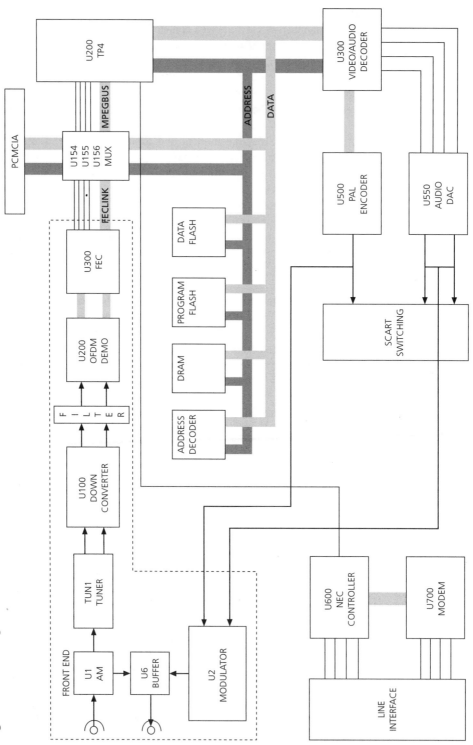

11 Interactive television

The term 'interactive television' covers a number of different applications. It covers any application that runs on an IRD which allows the user to control the behaviour of the application. This includes such diverse services as the electronic programme guide and teletext as well as home banking and video on demand. Home banking and video on demand require a return path to the service provider. It is this type of interactive television that will be considered here.

The return path may be an ordinary telephone line, an RF link or a network cable. Each requires an interface to facilitate communication between the set-top box and the physical medium. In the case of the telephone network, this may be a simple modem or a terminal adapter.

Interactive football which was first broadcast by BSkyB does not require a return path as all camera angles and statistical information that may be selected are incorporated within the transport stream with separate PES packets for each camera angle or text display. The demux extracts all relevant PESs but processes only those selected by the viewer. Since the inset video covers a small section of the screen, i.e. a small number of pixels, it requires a low bit rate. Fewer PES packets are therefore required compared with a full screen transmission. These PES packets are accommodated within the same channel and are extracted continuously but decoded and displayed only when selected by the remote control handset.

The modem interface

The modem interface is used where the medium of communication is the conventional telephone system and where only limited amounts of information are exchanged between the user and the service provider. Limited information exchange requires relatively low bit rates and is typical of *home banking* and *home shopping*.

Since a telephone channel is designed to carry analogue audio, i.e. speech signals, digital data from either end (the IRD or the service provider) must first be converted into a similar signal before it can be transmitted along a telephone channel. This involves modulating an audio carrier with digital data bits at one end and demodulating the carrier at the other end. Hence the need for a modulator/demodulator, modem, at either end of the telephone line (Fig.11.1). Digital data from the IRD is used to modulate an audio

Fig. 11.1   *Use of a modem and telephone line*

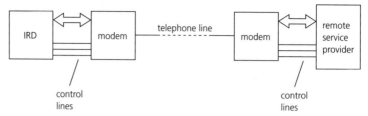

frequency carrier which may be sent via the telephone interface along the telephone line in the same way as an ordinary speech (audio) signal. Conversely, modulated carriers from a remote provider, normally known as a *head end*, are received by the modem, which converts them back to their original digital form.

Modem operation

Figure 11.2 shows the basic parts of a modem interface unit. A non-volatile memory chip such as an EEPROM is used to store modem settings as well as some software routines. Control of the modem and data transfer is carried out by the microprocessor.

When a remote broadcaster dials in, the telephone interface detects the incoming ring and seizes the line as if it had been answered by lifting the telephone receiver. A signal is then sent to alert the microprocessor to begin negotiating a connection. A process known as modem *handshaking* then commences which establishes an agreed protocol for communication and data exchange between the two modems. The protocol includes an agreed speed of transmission, the size of data packets, the number of signalling bits, parity or other error correction/detection techniques. Once a protocol is agreed, the controller sets up the modem and data exchange can begin. Dialling may be initiated by the IRD itself or by the broadcaster. The broadcaster may prompt the IRD to dial the head end by an off-air signal. Procedures are followed to ensure that dialling does not unduly interfere with the normal use of the telephone.

Fig. 11.2   *Modem interface*

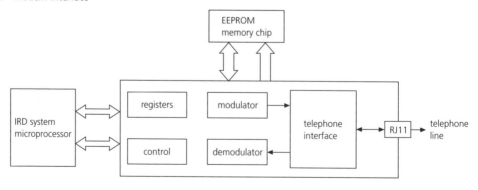

Bandwidth and speed

The bandwidth allocated for a telephone channel is 3 kHz (300 Hz to 3300 Hz). A data communication channel must therefore fit within this bandwidth. If communication is to take place in both directions simultaneously (*full-duplex* operation), the bandwidth of the telephone channel must be shared between the two-way signals using *frequency division multiplex (FDM)*, as shown in Fig. 11.3. Two different carrier frequencies are used, one for the transmit (Tx) channel and one for the receive (Rx) channel. These frequencies are generated by the modem itself. The modem originating the transmission generates the carrier for Tx, and the modem receiving the transmission generates the carrier for Rx. Each carrier is then modulated by the appropriate digital data and sent along the telephone line.

To ensure the integrity of the two-way communication, a gap is inserted between the two modulated signals (Fig. 11.3). This reduces the total available bandwidth to 2400 Hz: 1200 Hz for the Tx signals and 1200 Hz for the Rx signals. This means the maximum frequency that can be accommodated for full-duplex operation is 1200 Hz. Since maximum frequency is obtained when the transitions of the carrier alternate between 1 and 0 (Fig. 11.4) and since one cycle of the waveform represents two transitions (or bits), it follows that the rate of carrier transitions, i.e. the baud rate, is twice the bandwidth. This gives a maximum baud rate of 2 × 1200 = 2400. The actual bit rate is determined by the number of bits that each transition represents. For operation of 1 bit per baud, the maximum bit rate is 2400 bits per second (bps). Using QPSK, the bit rate may be doubled to 4800 bps, and so on. This explains why modem speed is a multiple of 2400 bps.

Fig. 11.3 *Full-duplex on a telephone channel needs FDM*

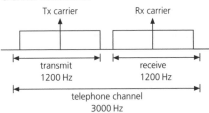

Fig. 11.4 *Maximum frequency occurs when carrier transitions alternate between 1 and 0*

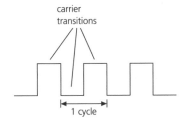

Modem standards

Before communication between two modems can commence, they have to establish a common communication protocol. A number of standard protocols for modems have been established (Table 11.1). They fall into two categories: the Microcom Networking Protocol (MNP) such as MNP class 2 and MNP class 3, and the Comité Consultatif International Télégraphique et Téléphonique (CCITT, International Telegraph and Telephone Consultative Committee) such as V.32 and V.42.

Figure 11.5 shows the basic components of a practical modem circuit employing digital signal processor DSP1675 V.34 (U700) used by Pace. U300 is the microprocessor chip and U802 is a DAC/ADC. The line interface provides the final connection to the telephone line. The line interface is fully controlled by U300 via a number of control signals (all active low):

- nottrigger (to check if line is available)
- nothook (to make connection)
- notdon (dial-on-network for pulse dialling)
- notsense (to sense condition on line).

U300 uses the standard address and data bus (MEMEDATA and MEMADDR) together with chip select (pin 11) and RD (pin 39) and WR (pin 40) to initialize and bring the modem into operation. Once the line interface is set up, dialling can take place and a line connection is obtained. Data may be exchanged along the telephone line via U802, the DAC/ADC chip. U802 has a number of registers that are used by the modem chip to set up its operating conditions via data line DOUT, clock IOCLK, SADD (serial address) and IOLD (input/output load).

When data is required to be sent to the service provider, it is first transferred to the modem DSP chip by U300 via the MEMDATA bus. The DSP converts the data from

Table 11.1 *Modem standards*	
Standard	Function
V.22	1200 bps at 600 baud using PSK
V.22bis	2400 bps at 600 baud using QAM
V.32	High speed data transfer of 4800 and 9600 bps at a baud rate of 2400 using QAM
V.32bis	Extends the V.32 to 4800, 7200, 12 000 and 14 000 bps at the same 2400 baud rate using TCQAM
V.32turbo	16 800, 19 200 bps with a baud rate of 2400
V.32fast	28 800 bps with 2400 baud rate
V.34	33.6 kbps
V.42	Error correction specification for V.32 and V.32bis incorporating MNP4
V.42bis	Error correction specification similar to but incompatible with MNP5 and MNP7
V.90	56 kbps

Fig. 11.5 *Pace circuit for a modem*

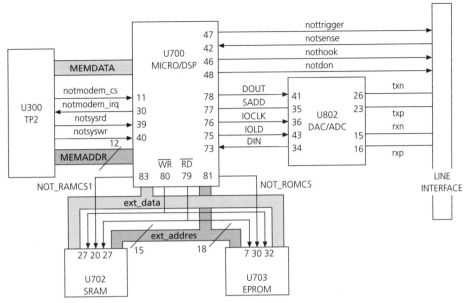

parallel to serial format and sends it to the DAC part of U802 via DOUT and IOCLK. The DAC converts the serial data into a differential analogue signal and transfers it to the line interface along balanced pair txn/txp. The process is reversed when data is sent by the provider to the set-top box. Analogue data arrives on balanced pair rxt/rxp, is converted into digital by the ADC part of U802 then sent to U700, which converts the serial data into a parallel format before sending it to U300.

Video on demand

The basic principle of *video on demand (VOD)* is very simple. Digitized video informa-tion stored on magnetic disks is retrieved by a video server and delivered to the home or office, where it is reconstructed using either a PC or an IRD and displayed on a television set. One approach to video distribution is to use a number of channels (typically ten) to broadcast the same video piece such as a film with starting times staggered by say 5–10 minutes. Known as *near video on demand (NVOD)*, this method will allow the viewer to choose the viewing time within specified limits. True video on demand allows the viewer full choice of viewing time, together with VCR-type controls such as fast forward, rewind, replay, and so on. Such specifications require a minimum bit rate in the region of 2 Mbit/s, forty times faster than the best performance of a V.90 modem. Hence the need for digital communication technology for use on existing telephone lines. This technology is *digital subscriber line (DSL)*. Designed to achieve high data trans-mission speeds over typical copper local telephone lines, DSL technology operates by using modulation techniques which exploit the fact that the simple twisted-pair wire used to connect a subscriber to the telephone exchange has a bandwidth far greater than

Fig. 11.6 *Data from the DSP modulates the pulse stream into analogue signals for the telephone channel*

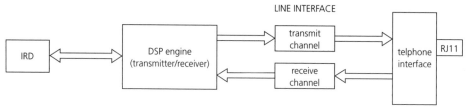

is needed for voice communication. Unlike the traditional modem, which encodes the digital information into tones, DSL uses digital signal processors (DSPs) and sophisticated analogue interfaces to transmit digital data at very high rates over the telephone wire. The data from the DSP is used to modulate the pulse stream into analogue symbols before going onto the telephone wire (Fig. 11.6). There are several DSL protocols available to subscribers. *ISDN*, a variant of DSL which provides two 64 kbit/s channels and one 9600 bit/s channel, has been widely used in the last decade or so. *Asymmetric DSL (ADSL)* is the most suitable for video applications. It provides two channels having different bit rate capacities (hence the name asymmetric): the downstream channel, from the provider to the subscriber, has a data rate of up to 8 Mbit/s and the upstream channel has a bit rate of up to 600 kbit/s for distances of up to 6 km. The downstream channel is used by the provider to send video and audio data, whereas the upstream channel is used by the subscriber to send individual requests to the provider. ADSL standard allows continued support for the normal voice telephone service alongside the digital data service.

Another technology for fast data transfer along a telephone wire is the *asynchronous transfer mode (ATM)* technology. Unlike ADSL, which provides a fixed bit rate capacity to a subscriber, ATM has the ability to automatically adjust the network capacity to meet the system needs and can support concurrent transmission of video, audio and other data traffic. ATM divides the data into small segments which are transported across the network within fixed 53-byte units called cells. All connections through which the cells travel to and from their destinations are based on virtual circuits, so called because the transmission path is not actually dedicated to an individual connection, but has sufficient resources statistically assigned to it as necessary. Before the start of any transmission, the ATM user interface negotiates a traffic contract, specifying the network, the data rate and the service quality required for the complete end-to-end virtual circuit. If the network is congested, requests for new connections can be refused, thus ensuring the negotiated quality is maintained for transmissions that are already in progress. ATM can operate at a bit rate of up to 622 Mbit/s.

A simple VOD system

Figure 11.7 illustrates the basic components of a VOD system. The video server contains storage devices and control mechanisms necessary to store video data in an MPEG compressed format to play it back on request. The storage devices may be RAM chips, hard disks or tapes. The server has access to a video library which contains the original video programmes. Apart from playback, the server has to perform a number of

Fig. 11.7 *A simple VOD system*

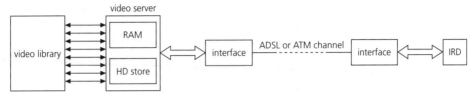

other functions, including admission control, request handling, data retrieval, guaranteed stream transmission, stream encryption and support for VCR-type functions. A basic requirement of a video server is to allow many users to view the same programme at different time instants. One way of achieving this is to have many identical copies of the programme with each individual programme serving one user. Another method is to use a technique known as *data striping*, in which the video information is divided into small chunks placed on different hard disks. When different users view the same programme or access different parts of the same programme at different instants, the video server can simultaneously retrieve different chunks of the video from different hard disks.

The process of requesting a video piece starts with a subscriber making a selection from a menu on the screen. This request is sent along the control channel to the server at the head end. The server authenticates the request, retrieves the data from the hard disk and feeds it to the telephone line via the interface. The interface is a terminal adapter which converts video and audio MPEG data into a form suitable for transmission along an ADSL or ATM channel to the subscriber.

The use of HDD

The use of hard disk drives for storing video information began to gain popularity as the size of HD increased and their price dropped. As a general rule, using MPEG-2 compression, about 2GB of storage capacity is needed for one hour of video and audio information.

HDD are incorporated in second-generation set-top-boxes, what is known as *extended television (XTV)*. They are also used in *personal video recorders (PVRs)* and other video-on-demand applications. In both cases, the principle is the same: MPEG bitstream consisting of audio and video and other PESs belonging to the selected programme is recorded directly onto the hard disk. On playback, the bitstream is read from the HD and sent to an MPEG A/V decoder to produce video and audio signals in the normal way. Both operations can take place simultaneously, a process known as time shifting. The HD thus handles two bitstreams, one for the live programme which is being recorded and a second for the delayed (time shifted) playback of the same programme. HDD recording is a random access medium and thus provides a number of other advantages over the linear VCR recording. With HDD there is no need to rewind or fast forward to move from one programme or part of a programme to another. The user can instantly skip to other programmes instantly. HDD medium provides more flexibility than simply speeding and reversing the programme. HDD supports multiple forward and reverse speeds by factors of ×10, ×20 and so on by using the index information provided by the HD filing system. It also allows the user to jump ahead or back to specific time intervals, features that are common in DVD applications.

Since the hard disk receives a direct digital signal from the tuner, the stored programme retains the original broadcast quality, which cannot be experienced on traditional video recorders. XTV and PVR are fully integrated in the broadcast system using smart software to select and store programmes. It enables personalised profiles of viewers' tastes and habits to be interpolated and stored so that recordings of favourite programmes may be made automatically.

12 Power supplies

A DTV integrated receiver decoder (IRD) requires a number of different stablized DC power lines. These include power for the tuner (33 V for tuning, 5 V for tuner RF and IF amplifiers), the channel decoder, audio amplifiers, SCART connector and various op-amps and ICs. All of these voltages have to be produced by the power supply section of the set-top box.

A simple power supply

A simple power supply (Fig. 12.1) consists of a mains transformer (T1) and a full-wave rectifier (D1/D2) which converts the mains waveform into a DC voltage with a large amount of 100 Hz ripple. To reduce the ripple, a reservoir capacitor C1 is used together with a lowpass filter R1/C2 with a cut-off frequency of 100 Hz. For more effective smoothing, the series resistor R1 may be replaced by a large inductor. In this simple circuit, the DC output decreases as the load current increases. Variations in the mains voltage will also produce changes in the output. For a constant DC output, a regulator or stabilizer must be used.

Fig. 12.1 *Unregulated power supply*

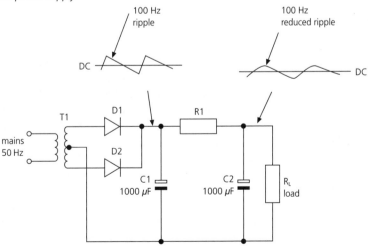

Fig. 12.2 *Series-stabilized power supply*

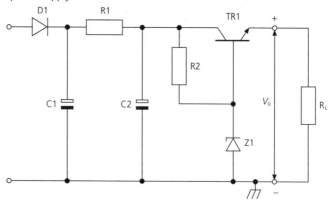

Fig. 12.3 *Shunt-regulated power supply*

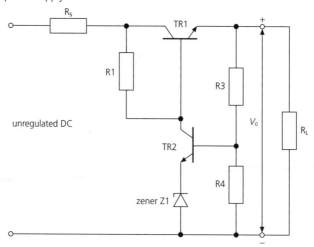

One method of stablizing the DC output is to use the series regulator shown in Fig. 12.2, where TR1 is the series regulator. Load regulation is obtained by zener diode Z1, which provides the reference voltage for the base of common emitter transistor TR1. Z1 maintains the base of TR1 at constant potential determined by its breakdown voltage. The DC taken at the emitter is thus maintained at 0.6 V below the zener voltage. Changes in the output level produce changes in the base–emitter bias of TR1 in such a way as to keep the output constant.

The sensitivity of the regulator may be improved by incorporating a voltage comparator, also known as an error detector. Figure 12.3 shows a simple regulator with TR2 acting as the error detector. TR2 compares the portion of the output voltage at the junction of R3/R4 with the reference voltage of zener Z1. Changes in the output voltage are amplified by TR2 and fed into the base of TR1 to maintain the output at a constant.

Switched-mode power supplies

The switched-mode power supply (SMPS) is in essence a converter. It converts unregulated DC into a switched or pulsating DC and back again into a regulated DC. The switching speed, typically a few hundred kilohertz, determines the ripple frequency at the output, making it easier to remove by a lowpass filter. The basic function blocks of an SMPS are shown in Fig. 12.4. The switching element, which may be a transistor or thyristor, is used to charge up a reservoir capacitor; it is opened and closed at regular intervals by a pulse from the control unit. The charge across the capacitor is determined by how long the switch is closed. Regulation is obtained by making the time intervals when the switching element is open and closed (i.e. the mark/space ratio of the control pulse) depend on the DC output. The control pulses may also be made to depend on the input voltage; this is to guard against changes in the mains (or battery) supply voltage.

The switching action of the switching element may involve large currents and may introduce interference known as mains pollution in the form of sharp transients, spikes or glitches superimposed upon the mains waveform. This is overcome by the introduction of high frequency chokes or decoupling capacitors at the input terminals; they prevent high frequency pulses from going back into the mains supply.

Control and regulation is only one requirement of the SMPS. The other requirement is efficient energy use, and this is achieved by using an inductor as an energy reservoir. The inductor may be connected in series or in parallel with the load. A series connection is shown in Fig. 12.5, where D1 acts as an efficiency diode. When the switching element S is closed, current I_1 flows from the positive side of the unregulated input into the load as shown. The magnetic field set up by the current flowing through L1 causes energy to be stored in the inductor. When the switch is open, the current ceases and the magnetic field collapses. A back EMF is induced across the inductor in such a way as to forward bias D1, causing a current I_2 to flow into the load in the same direction as before. The energy stored in the inductor when the switch was closed is therefore consumed when the switch is open. The ripple at the output has a frequency of twice the switching speed and is easily removed by smoothing capacitor C1.

A *shunt-type* SMPS is shown in Fig. 12.6. When switch S is closed, D1 is reverse biased and current I_1 flows into L1, feeding energy into the inductor. When the switch is open, I_1 collapses and the back EMF across the coil drives current I_2 into R_L,

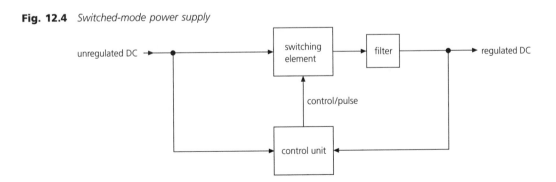

Fig. 12.4 *Switched-mode power supply*

Fig. 12.5 *SMPS: series type*

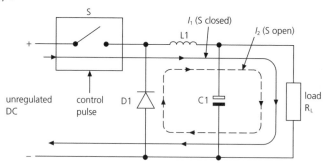

Fig. 12.6 *SMPS: shunt type*

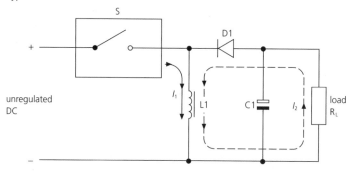

transferring the stored energy from the inductor to the load. One disadvantage of this technique is that, since the current flows into the load during the 'open' period of the switch, the output ripple is larger in amplitude and lower in frequency compared with the series connection. However, the parallel connection technique makes it possible to achieve electrical isolation by simply replacing the inductor with a transformer.

The self-oscillating SMPS

So far we have considered switched-mode power supplies with external pulses that control the switching elements. This may be avoided by introducing an oscillator whose frequency changes in such a way as to keep the DC output constant. A *blocking oscillator* (Fig. 12.7) is normally used. At switch-on, transistor TR1 begins to conduct as a result of the forward bias applied to its base via start-up resistor R1. The collector current increases, which induces a positive voltage across secondary winding S1. This forward biases D1 and further increases TR1 current. When saturation is reached, the increase in the current ceases and a negative voltage is induced across S1; this reverse biases D1 and switches off TR1. At this point, the voltage across primary winding P1 reverses and D2 switches on. The tuned circuit formed by primary winding P1 and C1 begins to oscillate, transferring energy from P1 to C1. For the second half of the cycle, when energy begins to transfer back to P1, diode D2 is reverse biased, oscillations stop and

Fig. 12.7 *Use of a blocking oscillator*

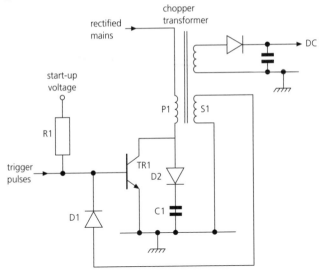

the current in P1 reverses; this causes a positive voltage to be induced across S1, turn-ing on TR1, and so on. Trigger pulses from the control circuit are used to initiate each cycle to keep the DC output constant.

Figure 12.8 shows a typical power supply for a terrestrial IRD. It provides 33 V, 16 V, 8 V, 5 V, −8 V and 3.3 V DC rails. Regulation is achieved by monitoring the 5 V rail with any variations being fed back to the self-oscillator/chopper U2 via optocoupler U3 to control its mark/space ratio and thus regulate the output. The mains voltage is full-wave rectified by bridge rectifier U1 and the resulting waveform is fed to reservoir capacitor C3 for smoothing. The DC output is then fed to the drain of MOSFET chopper/oscillator transistor U2 (pin 3) via primary winding of transformer T1, generating a small current at pin 1 which charges blocking capacitor C6. When the voltage across the capacitor goes above 4.7 V, the transistor begins to oscillate at about 100 kHz, gen-erating AC power into the primary of the transformer, and the DC power begins to build up. At this moment, the mark/space ratio of the oscillating waveform is at maximum. As the voltage on the 5 V rail builds up, a sample is fed to the LED of the optocoupler; it begins to conduct and this reduces the mark/space ratio. Stability will be achieved when the 5 V rail reaches its specified value. Should the voltage vary, the optocoupler LED will conduct more or less, and this in turn will alter the voltage applied to pin 1 of the MOSFET transistor, changing the mark/space ratio of the switching waveform and thus the DC output.

Fig. 12.8 Pace circuit for a DTV set-top box power supply

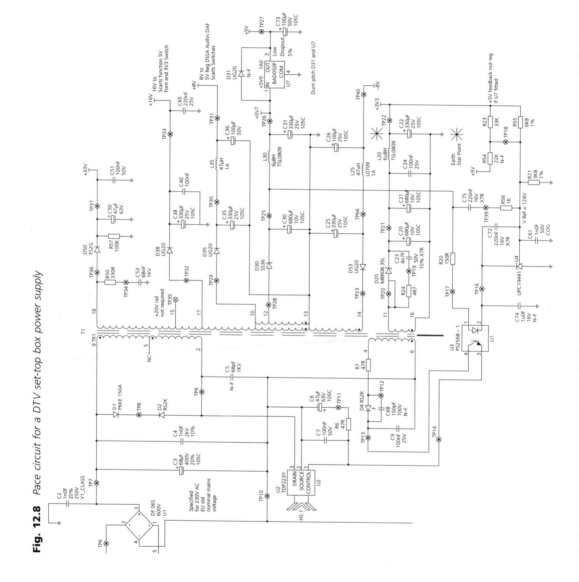

13 Testing DTV reception systems

The first step in attempting to service a suspect DTV system is to determine whether the fault lies within the set-top box (STB) or outside it. The external factors that affect the video display and its quality may be divided into two categories: those that precede the STB (*pre-STB*), such as aerial or dish alignment, aerial lead and signal strength, and those that succeed it (*post-STB*), such as the SCART connector and lead, the UHF output and the television set itself (Fig. 13.1). Failures caused by the first category may be total video/audio failure as well as break-up of video and/or sound, an effect peculiar to digital TV reception. Failures in the second category do not include this video/audio break-up.

Fig. 13.1 *Connecting the STB*

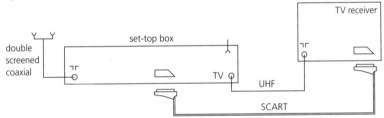

Aerials and dishes

In the conventional analogue system, low signal strength or low carrier-to-noise ratio (C/N) results in adverse picture quality, with ghosting in the case of terrestrial TV or noisy picture sparklies in the case of satellite TV. In digital TV reception such conditions would cause the picture and sound to fail altogether. Low signal strength would result in failure of the channel decoder to lock to a channel, with a message 'no signal' being displayed. In DTV the picture is either perfect or non-existent when the channel decoder fails to lock to a channel. This is known as the *digital cliff*.

Unlike conventional analogue reception, where low signal strength or low C/N would result in low signal amplitude, in DTV applications it would result in increased bit error rate (BER). If the BER is too high, the FEC unit cannot correct the errors and the data would be marked accordingly. The video decoder would normally decode PES packets and store the video information in the video memory before display. The video memory would thus be updated as new PES packets are decoded. However, when a PES is marked as erroneous, it is neglected and the relevant part of the video memory fails to update; this produces a *freeze* in that part of the picture and a picture break-up results. If a whole series of PES packets are marked erroneous, none of the video memory is updated and a picture freeze occurs. This effect can be seen if the signal is removed by removing the aerial lead. In this case the freeze continues for a few moments before the picture disappears completely. Where audio PES packets are marked erroneous, they are neglected by the audio decoder and sound break-up results.

A *spectrum analyser* may measure the strength of the signal from an antenna. However, care must be taken to ensure that the instrument has a wide enough bandwidth to provide an average reading of the strength of the whole signal. This is particularly important for DTTV reception. Detecting instruments with insufficient bandwidth would also produce wrong C/N ratio with an error margin as high as 10 dB. The minimum signal level for good domestic satellite reception is 47 dBμV. In the case of domestic terrestrial DTV reception, signal strength between 45 dBμV and 65 dBμV is necessary (compared with 60 and 80 dB for analogue TV broadcasting). Exceeding the upper limit would cause overloading by the analogue signal, resulting in picture and/or sound break up. As for the carrier-to-noise ratio, a C/N value greater than 26 dBμV and 9 dBμV is necessary for domestic terrestrial and satellite DTV reception respectively. In both cases, it is assumed that the installation is of a high standard, using double-screened coaxial cable, screened connectors, proper termination and good and well protected F connectors. This C/N figure of 26 dBμV for DTTV provides a margin of 6–7 dBμV for signal variation across the bandwidth, i.e. for a non-flat spectrum display. If the variation is more than 6–7 dBμV, then a higher C/N value is necessary. Kinks in the cable will affect the flatness of the spectrum and thus may cause errors resulting in picture and/or sound break-up.

The software resident within the STB provides a facility for measuring the signal strength which may be used as an indication of the signal strength but not as an accurate measurement.

Low signal strength may be caused by aerial misalignment, low antenna gain, or adverse reception conditions. Misalignment may be corrected using a spectrum analyser, which provides a display of the strength and quality in terms of the bit error ratio, (BER) or C/N ratio. By adjusting the terrestrial aerial or the satellite dish, the best position for maximum channel strength and quality may be obtained. A spectrum analyser is a bulky device that does not lend itself for use at the top of a ladder. For this reason, smaller and simpler detectors are used which provide an indication of the signal strength only that can be used to align the aerial or dish.

In terrestrial DTV reception, picture and/or sound break-up may also result from strong reflected waves with long delays. COFDM is designed to avoid the effects of reflected waves provided they arrive at the aerial before the end of the guard period. The actual time delay that may be accommodated will depend on the COFDM mode as well as the selected guard period. For a 2K mode and a guard period of one-quarter the symbol duration, the maximum delay that could be accommodated is 56 μs. Reflected waves with longer delays are normally too weak to have any effect on the decoding process. However, where high-gain aerials or RF amplifiers are used, these reflected waves with long time delays may be strong enough to introduce uncertainty in the FEC processor, resulting in intermittent video and/or sound break-up. To avoid this, plug-in attenuators may be fitted to the aerial input socket of the STB.

The aerial cable carries signals with frequencies in the UHF or higher bands. Cable attenuation and the physical condition of the lead thus become important factors in signal integrity. This explains why low impedance double-screened coaxial cables are normally used. Bends and kinks in the cable may disturb the standing wave along the cable, causing intermittent video and/or sound break-up. Similar effects may be produced if the cable is squeezed by a very tight clip for instance.

For satellite reception, the size of the dish, the condition of the F-connectors and the condition of the LNB will have an effect on the signal strength and hence the quality of the video reproduction.

Post-STB fault conditions

At the other end of the STB, picture and/or audio failure may be caused by loose SCART connection or bad SCART cable. A failure on one or more pins of the SCART connector may cause failure of video and/or sound. To confirm a suspected SCART malfunction, the DTV programme may be viewed using the UHF modulator output. A good video/audio confirms a faulty SCART section, including the SCART cable, the connectors at either end and the interfaces at the STB and the television receiver. The SCART connection may also be tested by a VCR programme.

Where the STB is connected to the TV set via its UHF output, malfunction may be caused by failure to tune the TV set to the correct channel or failure to select the correct channel, as well as loose aerial connection or bad aerial lead between the STB and TV set. Failure within the TV set itself may be confirmed by selecting and viewing an analogue or VCR channel.

Patterning on the video is normally caused by incorrect RF modulator frequency at other devices connected to the same RF chain, such as a VCR. To check this, remove the VCR from the RF signal chain and observe the effect on the digital TV channel.

Tuning

Modern DTV boxes provide automatic channel tuning. This is carried out by accessing a standard menu; by selecting the appropriate items, a user may instruct the STB to search for all available channels, identify them, allocate appropriate programme numbers and store the information in memory. A facility for manual tuning may also be provided to allow the installer to check and set the frequency, polarization, symbol rate and FEC ratio of any channel.

The boot-up sequence

Normally a set-top box is never switched off. When not in use, it remains in the standby mode. Its microprocessor, microcontroller and all other processing chips remain set and ready to receive and process data.

However, when an STB is switched on from cold, the reset pin of the microprocessor goes high and the microprocessor searches for the start-up program by placing the start-up address on the address bus (Fig. 13.2). This address is the start of the *start-up*

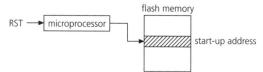

routine stored in flash memory. The processor then goes through a comparatively lengthy process of setting, initializing, configuring and programming the processor and decoder chips. This requires the loading of the operating platform (also known as the *start-up program*) and other software routines from flash memory to the microprocessor DRAM memory. This process is known as the start-up or boot-up sequence. The boot-up sequence consists of two parts: boot-loader and initialization. The boot-loader process involves reading and loading the start-up program and checking the applications. If the boot-loader finds any corrupt programs or applications, it will attempt to download new software off-air. This will only succeed if the box has been set up correctly so that connection to the provider can be made via a satellite dish or a terrestrial aerial.

An off-air software download is indicated by the LED display on the front panel of the digital box. Download progress may also be observed on a TV screen if the box is connected to the TV set via a SCART cable. If the boot-loader process is completed successfully, the onboard processor carries out the next phase – box initialization. This involves the processor checking that it can communicate with all other processing devices, including the memory chips, video/audio decoder, modem, smart card and conditional access module, and initialize them by loading the appropriate data into their registers.

If the initialization phase fails and the process goes no further than the boot-loader, the STB will remain stuck at standby. This is the most common fault of a DTV box. The cause could be faulty microprocessor or corrupt flash software or hardware malfunction. Testing micro reset, address and date lines at switch-on would give a clear indication of the health of the microprocessor itself. If the flash software is corrupted, attempt a forced upgrade. Alternatively, flash memory chips may be reprogrammed by a PC via an RS-232 or SCSI port. If an upgrade fails, the flash memory which holds the boot-up software must be suspected. A new set of programmed flash memory chips may then be used to replace the suspected set. If hardware malfunction is suspected, the actual faulty chip must be found and replaced; the procedure depends on the chipset. A first step would be to check the I²C bus for activity at all the chips during the boot-up process.

If the initialization process is completed successfully, the channel decoder begins to search for the default channel, known as the *home channel*. If the signal is detected, the channel decoder locks to it, data is received, decoded and processed. Picture and sound are produced. If the home channel cannot be detected, the channel decoder searches for other channels. Failure to lock to any incoming signal is indicated by a 'no signal' message on the screen.

Testing the set-top box

For the purpose of servicing, a digital TV receiver/decoder may divided into two parts (Fig. 13.3):

Fig. 13.3 *DTV IRD: analogue and digital parts*

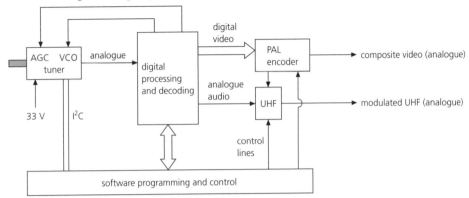

- An analogue part comprising the tuner at the front end, the PAL encoder and UHF modulator at the back end as well as other analogue applications such as audio amplifiers and the power supply.
- A digital part comprising digital decoding and processing (demodulation, FEC, demultiplexing, video/audio decoding), software programming and control and other devices such as address decoders, ADCs and DACs.

A fault in either part may cause partial or total failure of video and/or audio signals. The process of faultfinding involves identifying the faulty stage, e.g. the front end, the video/audio decoder or the PAL encoder, and having done that, proceed to identify the cause of the fault such as a malfunction serial bus or a clock failure. Initial symptoms such as mosaic display or complete audio malfunction may give an indication as to possible faulty stages. It is, however, necessary to carry out signal tests to isolate the faulty stage. Signal tests include signal tracing, but in the case of DTV decoders it is more important to test the control signals.

Signal tracing involves testing both analogue signals and digital data streams at regular points along the signal path. Analogue signals are normally tested by an oscilloscope whereas digital signals and control signals may be tested by a logic probe or a storage oscilloscope.

Use of the logic probe

The *logic probe* (Fig. 13.4) is a logic state test instrument which indicates the logic state at a test node. It can indicate logic 1, logic 0, an open circuit and a data stream pulse. Two indicator LEDs are used to indicate a high and a low. An open circuit or indeterminate logic state is indicated by no light. The presence of digital activity in the form of a bitstream is indicated by a flickering light or a special indicator. By the use of a pulse stretcher, pulses as narrow as 10 ns may be detected. Although the actual waveform cannot be examined by the logic probe, it nonetheless provides a fast and simple method of testing for digital activity at various points along the signal path. Where real-time waveforms have to be examined, an oscilloscope has to be used. DTV applications require a logic probe with a bandwidth of at least 100 MHz.

Fig. 13.4 *Logic probe*

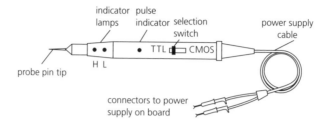

Use of the cathode ray oscilloscope

The *oscilloscope* is used to display both analogue and digital waveforms from which measurements of amplitude, frequency and time can then be made. Analogue signals in a digital decoder box are not dissimilar to those found on an analogue TV receiver and may be displayed using a normal analogue oscilloscope. However, examining a data bitstream requires a digital storage oscilloscope with a minimum bandwidth of 100 MHz and a sampling rate of 500 million samples per second. Such an oscilloscope may also be used to display and examine analogue signals.

The *storage oscilloscope* captures a part of the data bitstream, stores it and then displays the waveform on the screen for examination and measurements. This may then be repeated for another part of the data stream, and so on. Unlike analogue systems, where a test point has its own unique signal in terms of waveform, frequency and amplitude, a sequence of 1s and 0s in a data stream has the same general waveform and amplitude regardless of the test point (Fig. 13.5).

In microprocessor-based systems, failure may occur due to wrong or missing clock signals or due to incorrect timing of address, data and control signals. A fault in timing or synchronization can result in partial or total failure of the system. The timing and synchronization of the various data and control bitstreams may be examined using a multi-trace oscilloscope which displays two or more signals simultaneously. Figure 13.5

Fig. 13.5 *Multichannel digital storage scope: typical display*

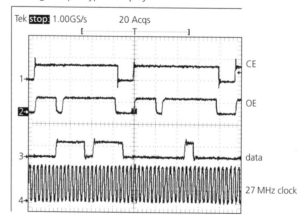

shows a typical multi-trace display illustrating the time relationship between chip select (CS), read or output enable (OE), a data line and the clock of a memory chip.

Testing the tuner

The function of the tuner (Fig. 13.6) is to downconvert, amplify, filter and demodulate the transmitted signal to reproduce the digitally modulated carrier. The local oscillator is controlled by the VCO DC voltage from the demodulator. When the decoder is turned on, it attempts to lock to the default channel known as the home channel. If it fails to do so, a search sawtooth waveform is fed into the VCO input pin (Fig. 13.7). At the same time, the AGC input is set to provide maximum tuner gain. If the tuner locks to another channel, the search stops and the VCO signal trace changes to a DC of 8–15 V. If the trace continues to display a sweep, then the channel set-up (frequency, polarization, symbol rate and FEC ratio) should be checked. If this does not cure the problem, activities on the serial I²C bus should be checked using a logic probe. If there is no activity, the AGC voltage should be checked before the tuner itself is suspected. LNB supply switching voltages may be tested using a *digital voltmeter (DVM)*.

Fig. 13.6 *Testing the tuner*

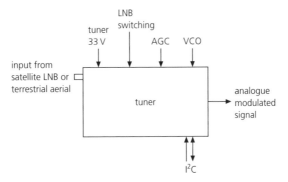

Fig. 13.7 *Using a search sawtooth on the VCO input*

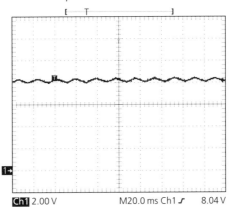

Testing the channel decoder

The modulated carrier entering the channel decoder is in the form of two quadrature carriers: *I* and *Q* in the case of satellite transmission (Fig. 13.8) and COFDM carriers in the case of terrestrial transmission (Fig. 13.9). The function of the channel decoder is to digitize the incoming carriers into a multi-bit stream, demodulate them and reproduce error-free MPEG packets.

Testing a satellite channel decoder should start with checking the dual-ADC sampling clock, which is normally set to twice the symbol rate (thus a rate of 27.5 million symbols per second will result in a sampling rate of 55 MHz). The sampling clock should be present regardless of whether the tuner is locked to a channel. A missing sampling clock pulse or a wrong frequency would cause a complete malfunction of the channel decoder. If the sampling clock is present and correct, other signals should be tested, commencing with the output MPEG packets. This is carried out by examining the MPEG data lines, line by line, using a logic probe or an oscilloscope. With no MPEG packets present, control signals MPEGSTART, MPEGCLOCK and DATAVALID should be tested. All should indicate digital activities. MPEGCLOCK may be calculated as $2 \times$ symbol rate $\times$ FEC rate $\times \frac{1}{8}$; for a symbol rate of 27.5 million symbols per second, MPEGCLOCK is 4.58 MHz. MPEGFAIL should indicate a DC voltage of around

Fig. 13.8 *Testing the channel decoder: satellite*

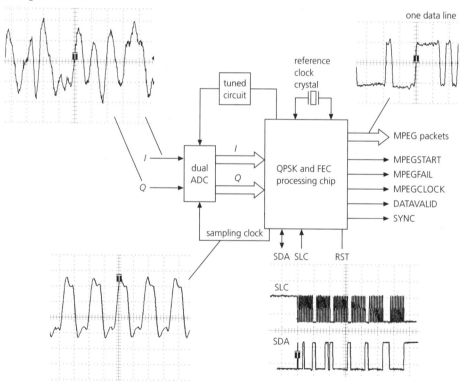

Fig. 13.9 *Testing the channel decoder: terrestrial*

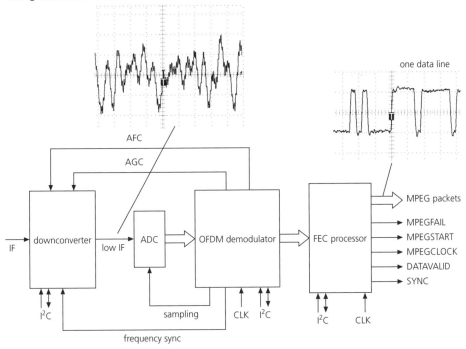

3.3 V. SYNC indicates high (3.3 V) if the channel decoder is locked to a channel. The serial bus should also be tested by a logic probe or storage oscilloscope while changing channels. Typical waveforms are illustrated in Fig. 13.8. Testing for *I* and *Q* signals provides no clear indication of whether or not a signal is present. Hence the need to test the control signals.

Testing a terrestrial channel decoder (Fig. 13.9) should follow a similar pattern to testing a satellite channel decoder. The sampling clock of the ADC should be checked first. It is normal to have an 18 MHz clock pulse with an amplitude of around 4 V. Further checks involve testing the MPEG packets at the output of the FEC processor chip, at the output of the OFDM demodulator and at the output of the ADC. All data lines should indicate digital activities on a logic probe or an oscilloscope. Typical waveforms are illustrated in Fig. 13.9.

Here are some of the control signals and their properties for satellite and terrestrial channel decoders:

- MPEGSTART: high for the first byte of each packet
- MPEGFAIL: low if the packet contains errors
- DATAVALID: high for 188 bytes of the packet and low for the following 16 bytes
- SYNC: high if synchronization is correct
- Reset (RST): permanently high if active low, and vice versa
- SCL (clock line of the I²C control bus): a clock pulse
- SDA (data line of the I²C control bus): data stream pulse

Testing processing and decoding chips

Here is the general procedure to test processing and decoding chips:

- The input and output data streams
- The processing and other clocks
- Microprocessor control and communication signals
- Memory data/address bus and control signals

Demultiplexer

Figure 13.10 shows the demultiplexing part of the transport processor SoC. The input to the transport demultiplexer is MPEG data packets together with control signals MPEGSTART, MPEGFAIL and MPEG clock from the channel decoder via the descrambler. The function of the demux is to reassemble the video and audio packets of the selected programme in the correct order and send them to the V/A decoder via the data and address buses. The same bus structure is used to access the fast memory SRAM chips. Testing the demux involves checking the control signals from the channel decoder followed by the demux chip clock and the 27 MHz system clock. The presence of a clock pulse may be tested by a logic probe. However, an accurate measurement of the frequency has to be made using an oscilloscope or a frequency meter to ensure the correct value. An inaccurate clock frequency would cause total failure of the processor chip. A faulty clock pulse should be traced back through the clock-generating circuitry to ascertain the faulty component. A 27 MHz *system clock generator* is shown in Fig. 13.11.

Fig. 13.10 *Testing the transport processor*

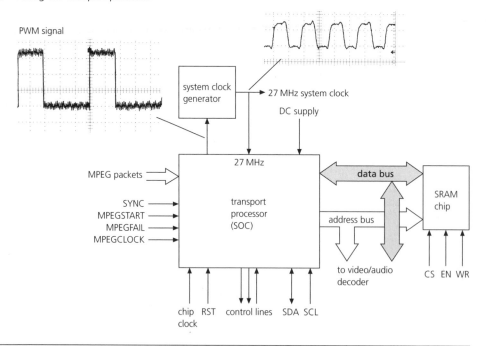

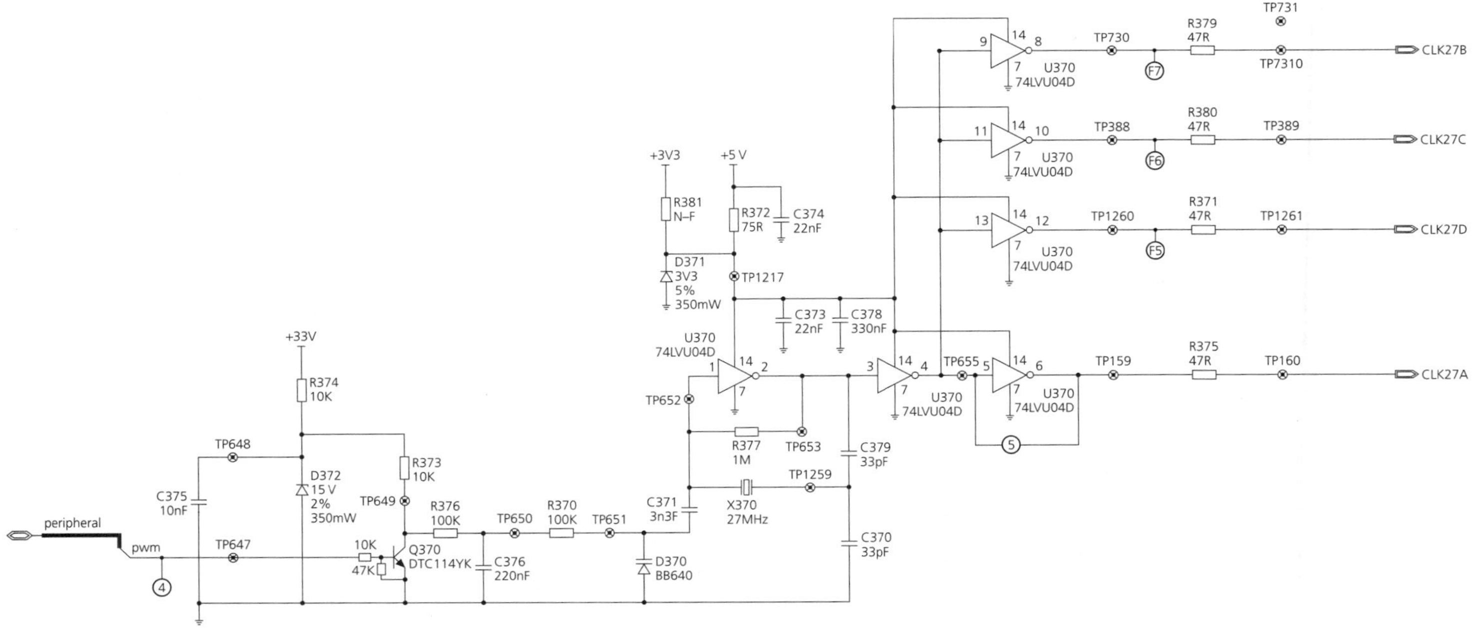

Fig. 13.11 *Pace circuit for a 27 MHz pixel clock generator*

The demux extracts the programme clock reference (PCR) data from the transport stream and generates a pulse width modulated (PWM) waveform to control the clock generator. The PWM signal is fed into transistor Q370, which turns on and off in accordance with the mark/space ratio of the PWM signal. A high mark/space ratio produces a low collector voltage, and vice versa. The output at the Q370 collector is first smoothed by lowpass T-type filter R376-C376-R370. The smoothed DC voltage is then used to control the capacitance of the varicap diode D370 which synchronizes the frequency of the crystal-controlled oscillator U370-x370-C370-C371-D370. The 27 MHz clock is then buffered and split into four separate outputs using NOR gates (U370).

The transport processor control signals should be tested for three kinds of digital activity:

- Reset (should be permanently high)
- SCL (clock line of I²C bus)
- SDA (data line of I²C bus)

SRAM memory chips may be tested by checking for digital activity along their data and address lines plus the read or output enable (OE), write enable (WE) and chip enable (CE) control lines. Figure 13.10 shows a typical PWM waveform from the transport processor to the system clock generator; it also shows the expected 27 MHz system clock.

Video/audio decoder and PAL encoder

The video/audio decoder (Fig. 13.12) has two functions:

- To convert the MPEG video packets from the demux into multiplexed Y, C_R and C_B data suitable for the PAL encoder.
- To convert audio MPEG packets into PCM serial data suitable for processing by a DAC.

The input and output data streams may be tested using a logic probe to check for digital activity, or an oscilloscope to display real-time waveforms. The input MPEG data is fed via the microprocessor data bus. The video output is in the form of an 8-bit multiplexed output Y, C_R and C_B. The audio output is in the form of a serial L/R multiplexed PCM digital stream. The multiplexing order is determined by an L/R control signal having a frequency equal to the audio sampling. The 27 MHz system clock and the decoder processing clock should be checked next, followed by the control signals which regulate the transfer of data between the demux and the decoder: VIRQ (video interrupt request) and VSTROB (video strobe), AUDIRQ (audio interrupt request), AUDSTROB (audio strobe) and the audio sampling rate. Depending on the chip, other control signals may be present such as VREQ (video request) and AUDREQ (audio request), not to be confused with video and audio interrupt requests. VREQ and AUDREQ go high (3.3 V) and remain high when the A/V chip is fully initialized and ready to receive video and audio packets.

SDRAM (synchronous DRAM) memory may be tested by checking the chip's data, address and control lines in the normal way. Testing the PAL encoder involves checking the input and output signals. Table 13.1 is a typical list of these signals and their types. The input to the audio ADC consist of a sampling clock, a PCM clock, L/R control and a PCM data line. All signals may be checked by a logic probe for digital activity or an oscilloscope for real-time waveforms. The output of the ADC is a two-channel

Fig. 13.12 *Testing the video/audio decoder*

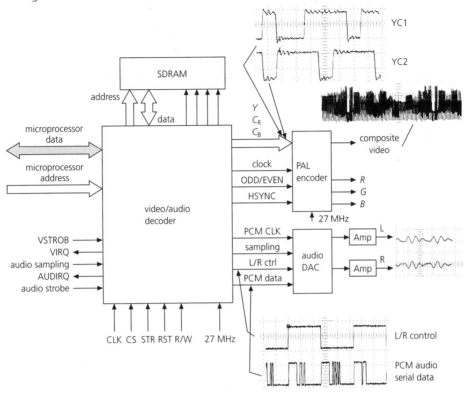

Table 13.1 *Check these signals at the PAL encoder*	
Signal	**Type**
Composite video signal	analogue
RGB colour signals	analogue
Video clock from the decoder	analogue/digital
27 MHz system clock	analogue/digital
Field sync (odd/even)	analogue
Horizontal sync (HSYNC)	analogue

analogue sound signal, and it may be checked with a simple analogue oscilloscope. Typical waveforms are shown in Fig. 13.12.

Testing the UHF modulator

Figure 13.13 shows a circuit diagram for a Pace satellite modulator/loop-through section. U640 is a synthesized UHF tuner which generates RF outputs to two TV aerial sockets, TV1 OUT and TV2 OUT. Composite video (CVBS) and mono audio are fed into pins

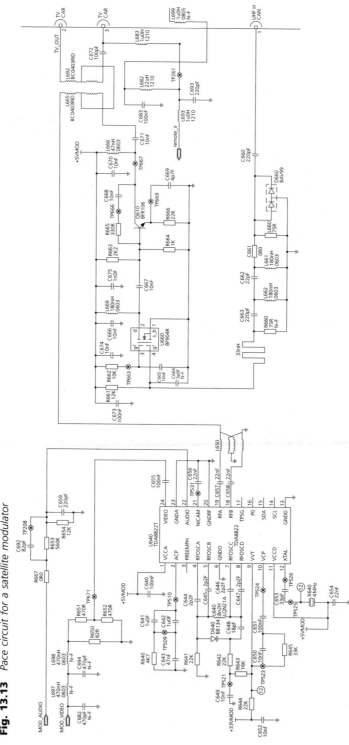

Fig. 13.13 *Pace circuit for a satellite modulator*

24 and 22 respectively. The modulator is controlled by the I^{2}C control bus (pins 14 and 15), which sets the UHF modulating frequency, and a balanced UHF output is produced at pins 18 and 19. UHF signal from an external terrestrial aerial goes into UHF IN and loops through amplifiers U660 and Q610, then mixes with the modulator RF signal to appear at the TV OUT sockets.

Examining a suspect chip

The absence of an output from a processing chip does not necessarily mean that the chip is faulty. In a microprocessor-based system, IC output failure may result from one of several malfunctions, including a clock pulse, a control signal, a software routine, data or address bus lines, a memory chip, a DC supply line as well as a faulty IC itself. In general, before a suspect IC is replaced, the following items should be checked:

- Check the IC is receiving its DC supply voltage at the appropriate pins; if not, then the DC line should be traced back to the power supply to ascertain the fault.
- Check it is operating at the correct frequency; this may be checked on a suitable oscilloscope. Where more than one clock pulse is fed into the chip, all pulses must be checked in the same way.
- Check it is receiving the correct instructions from the microprocessor or the microcomputer, or both. This means checking the I^{2}C bus lines, the control signals and the data and address lines.
- Check that the necessary software is valid and up to date.

The DC check may be carried out using a DVM to measure the DC voltage at the appropriate pins of the chip. The clock signal may be checked using an oscilloscope with adequate frequency range. The clock pulse must have

- The correct frequency
  – calculated from the periodic time of the waveform
- A fast-rising square shape
- An amplitude of 3.5 to 5.25 V
  – normally around 4.8 V

Checking hardware control lines involves using a logic probe to check for digital activity, or a storage oscilloscope to examine the actual waveforms of the various control signals such as chip select (CS), acknowledge (ACK), read, write, strobe and interrupt. The reset (RST) may be tested by a logic probe or a DVM. It is normally active low, i.e. it resets the chip when it is taken low and restarts when taken high. If it is active low then the RST line should be permanently high. The signals at the data and address lines may be examined for digital activity using a logic probe or an oscilloscope.

The bitstream may also be interrupted by faulty software such as out-of-date, deleted or corrupted programs. Software processing routines are mainly stored in flash memory chips. Rewriting or upgrading the software can be carried out off-air, or by using a personal computer which communicates with the decoder via a serial port using an RS-232 cable. The PC is then used to program the flash memory with up-to-date software routines. Alternatively, the flash memory chip may be replaced with a fully programmed chip.

Testing the programming and control

A malfunction in the programming and control section, i.e. the microprocessor, micro-controller and associated memory chips and components, will normally cause the start-up routine to be halted and this leads to a fatal video and audio fault.

A quick and reliable test of the programming and control section is the *menu test*. A menu displayed on the screen is a positive indication that this section is functioning normally. It also indicates that the A/V decoder and all subsequent units are function-ing normally.

Testing the chips for malfunction involves testing for digital activities on the address, data and control lines during and after the start-up sequence using either a logic probe or a storage oscilloscope. No activity at all suggests a DC supply failure or reset malfunction. Fatal malfunction may be caused by inaccurate clock frequency. Before the microprocessor is replaced, the chip clock frequency should be measured using an oscilloscope or a frequency meter. A small drift would cause the processor to cease operation.

Apart from a malfunctioning microprocessor or microcontroller system, certain faults in the demultiplexer and decoder chips can also cause the start-up sequence to be halted.

Testing logic devices

DTV receivers include a large variety of logic devices such as gates, flip-flops, counters and inverters. Such devices may be tested for *stuck-at faults* (stuck-at one when a pin is shorted to the supply line and stuck-at zero when a pin is shorted to the 0 V line) and open-circuit (o/c) faults. These faults are normally caused by a failure within the IC itself. Stuck-at and o/c faults may be detected using a *logic pulser* in conjunction with a logic probe.

The logic pulser changes the logic state of an IC pin or test point and then changes it back again, i.e. it drives a low node high and then low, and a high node low and then high. Testing a logic device, such as a gate, takes the form of stimulating the inputs using the pulser and observing the effect on the output using the logic probe. For example, consider the simple steering network which is used to set the read (RD) and write (WR) control signals for a modem. A quad NAND gate 7400 package is used as shown in Fig. 13.14. NAND gate U511A may be tested by placing the pulser at pin 2 and monitoring the output at pin 3 with a logic probe. Since the second input to the gate (pin 1) is at +5 V, changing the state of pin 2 will result in a change in the output at pin 3; this will be indicated by a flicker on the probe. No indication on the probe suggests a faulty pin 2 or pin 3. The process can be repeated for the other gates until the faulty pin is identified. The stuck-at fault may be confirmed by placing both the pulser and probe on the suspect pin. The fault is confirmed if the operation of the pulser does not result in a flicker on the probe.

Once an IC pin is identified as stuck at zero or stuck at one, establish the source of the short circuit to earth (stuck at zero) or the short circuit to the DC supply voltage (stuck at one). For instance, if in Fig. 13.14, pin 8 is found to be stuck at zero, then

Fig. 13.14 *Simple steering network for a modem*

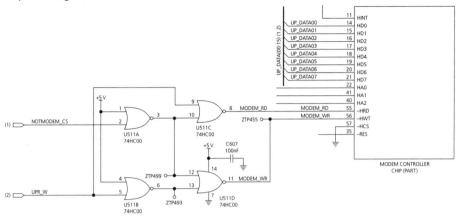

either pin 8 of the 7400 chip is shorted to earth or pin 55 (MODEM_RD) of the modem controller is shorted to earth. Identifying the cause of the fault requires a very sensitive ohmmeter or a *current tracer* in conjunction with a pulser. The current tracer senses the magnetic field created by the flow of fast-rising pulses and indicates their presence by an indicator light or constant-tone sound. Before a current tracer is used, power must be switched off. The pulser is then placed at one of the suspect pins (say pin 8 of the AND gate in Fig. 13.14). If the actual short circuit is at pin 55 of the modem controller chip, pulses from the pulser will flow from pin 8 to pin 55. The current can then be used to detect the presence of the current at pin 55. However, if the short circuit is at pin 8, the current tracer will detect no current at pin 55.

Memory faults

Table 13.2 outlines the functions of memory chips in a DTV box. Memory chips may fail either totally or partially. Partial failure may be caused by corruption of one or more cells; an address, data or control pin stuck at low or high; or shorted pins. Table 13.3 lists some symptoms caused by memory faults.

Table 13.2 *Memory chips and their function*

Memory	Function
DRAM	Microprocessor temporary memory store
Flash	Microprocessor permanent memory for storing boot-up and other routines
SRAM (static RAM)	Demux memory for storing relevant PESs
Video/audio SDRAM (synchronous DRAM)	Video memory store and audio delay

Table 13.3 Memory faults and resulting symptoms

Memory	Partial failure	Total failure	Comments
DRAM	Stuck at standby	Stuck at standby	Boot-up and other routines will not be downloaded from flash
Flash	Stuck at standby	Stuck at standby	Absence of boot-up routine
SRAM	Constantly changing pattern of picture break-up Menu normal	No picture or sound Menu display normal	The picture breaks up in blocks rather than pixels as wrong PESs are decoded
V/A SDRAM	Constantly changing pattern of picture break-up and sampled sound Menu normal	No picture or sound Menu display normal	Picture break-up is in the form of pixelization as pixels are displayed in the wrong position on the screen

Fault diagnosis flow charts

Faultfinding flow charts provide a generalized step-by-step approach to fault diagnosis for a given symptom. It is neither possible nor desirable to construct a flow chart for all fault symptoms. Although faultfinding is a logical process, it is very much down to the individual and depends a great deal on previous experience. Here are flow charts for two of the most common fault symptoms: stuck at standby and the screen message 'no signal'.

Stuck at standby

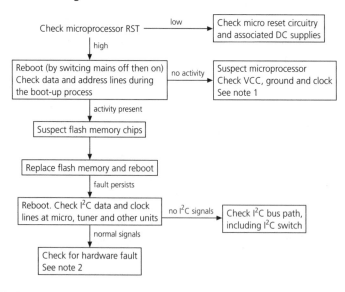

No signal: satellite decoder

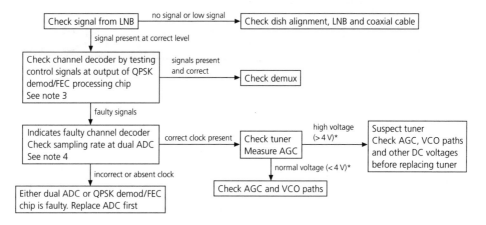

No signal: terrestrial decoder

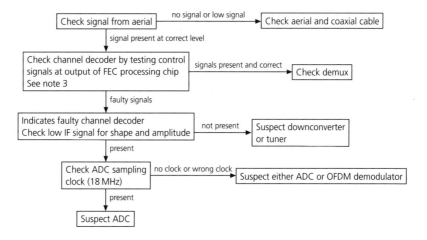

Notes

1. The clock must be within ±5% of the stated value.
2. Hardware faults could include the various processing chips as well as logic chips such as gates, address decoders and comparators.
3. Control signals include MPEG start pulse, clock, valid and fail.
4. The sampling clock should be 2 × the symbol rate. For BSkyB in the UK, the symbol rate is 27.5 million symbols per second, so the sampling rate is 55 MHz.
* These are only approximate values; actual voltages will depend on the make of the set-top box.

Appendix A
MPEG-2 profiles and levels

Level \ profile	simple	main	SNR	spatial	high
High		4:2:0 1920 × 1152 80 Mbit/s I, P, B			4:2:0, 4:2:2 1920 × 1152 100 Mbit/s I, P, B
High-1440		4:2:0 1440 × 1152 60 Mbit/s I, P, B		4:2:0 1440 × 1152 60 Mbit/s I, P, B	4:2:0, 4:2:2 1440 × 1152 80 Mbit/s I, P, B
Main	4:2:0 760 × 576 15 Mbit/s I, P	4:2:0 720 × 576 15 Mbit/s I, P, B	4:2:0 720 × 576 15 Mbit/s I, P, B		4:2:0, 4:2:2 720 × 576 20 Mbit/s I, P, B
Low		4:2:0 352 × 288 4 Mbit/s I, P, B	4:2:0 352 × 288 4 Mbit/s I, P, B		

Appendix B
Broadcasting stations for satellite DTV

Figure B.1 shows a variety of broadcast satellites. The table lists digital television channels broadcast from the Astra 2A 28.2° satellite. For each transponder it states the bouquet name, frequency, polarity, transponder number, encryption type, symbol rate and FEC rate, along with the approximate minimum dish sizes for south (London) and north (Edinburgh).

Fig. B1

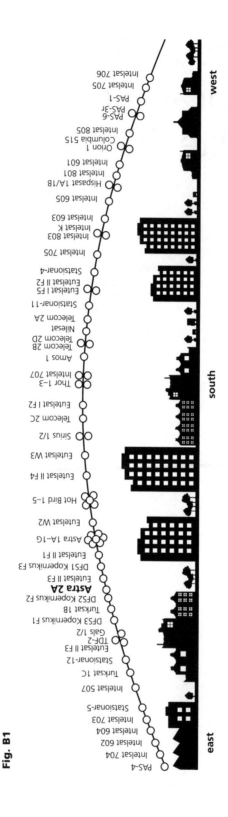

west

Intelsat 706
Intelsat 705
PAS-1
PAS-3r
PAS-6
Intelsat 805
Columbia 515
Orion 1
Intelsat 601
Intelsat 801
Hispasat 1A/1B
Intelsat 605
Intelsat 603
Intelsat K
Intelsat 803
Intelsat 705
Statsionar-4
Eutelsat II F2
Eutelsat I F5
Statsionar-11
Telecom 2A
Nilesat
Telecom 2D
Telecom 2B
Amos 1
Intelsat 707
Thor 1–3
Eutelsat I F2
Telecom 2C
Sirius 1/2
Eutelsat W3
Eutelsat II F4
Hot Bird 1–5
Eutelsat W2
Astra 1A–1G
Eutelsat II F1
DFS1 Kopernikus F3
Eutelsat II F3
Astra 2A
DFS2 Kopernikus F2
Turksat 1B
DFS3 Kopernikus F1
Gals 1/2
TDF-2
Eutelsat II F3
Statsionar-12
Turksat 1C
Intelsat 507
Statsionar-5
Intelsat 703
Intelsat 604
Intelsat 602
Intelsat 704
PAS-4

south

east

Sky Digital 11.720H Tp1 Videoguard 27500 2/3 Sth45cm Nth60cm

BBC1	General entertainment	English
BBC2	General entertainment	English
BBC Choice	General entertainment	English
BBC News 24	General entertainment	English
BBC1 NI	General entertainment	English
BBC Knowledge	General entertainment	English

Sky Digital 11.740V Tp2 Videoguard 27500 2/3 Sth45cm Nth60cm

Living	Women's TV	English
Challenge TV	Games shows	English
Trouble	Teen TV	English
Bravo	Bloke TV	English
Sky Box Office	PPV channels	English
Sky Movie Max 2	Films	English
Sky Premier 2	Films	English
Sky Sports News	Sports news	English
National Geographic	Documentaries	English

Sky Digital 11.876H Tp9 Videoguard 27500 2/3 Sth45cm Nth60cm

Discovery Channel	Documentaries	English
Animal Planet	Documentaries	English
Home & Leisure	DIY and fishing	English
Discovery +1	Documentaries	English
Travel & Adventure	Exploration	English
Discovery Sci-Trek	Technology	English
Discovery Civilization	History	English

Sky Digital 11.895V Tp10 Videoguard 27500 2/3 Sth45cm Nth60cm

MTV	Music	English
VH-1	Music	English
M2	Music	English
Paramount Comedy	Comedy classics	English
Nick Junior	Children's shows	English
Sci-Fi Channel	SF and horror	English
MTV Extra	Music	English
MTV Base	Music	English
VH-1 Classic	Music	English

Sky Digital 11.914H Tp11 Videoguard 27500 2/3 Sth45cm Nth60cm

Sky Box Office	PPV channels	English
Sky Movie Max 3	Films	English
Sky Premier 3	Films	English
Sky Digital Info	Info	English
Sky Sports 3	Sports	English

Sky Digital 11.934V Tp12 Videoguard 27500 2/3 Sth45cm Nth60cm

Sky Box Office	PPV channels	English
Sky Movie Max 4	Films	English
Sky Premier 4	Films	English
Playboy/Adult Channel	Erotic	English
Sky Digital Retail	Info	English

Sky Digital 11.954H Tp13 Videoguard 27500 2/3 Sth45cm Nth60cm

Screenshop	Home shopping (clear)	English
TV-X	Erotic	English
TV Travel Shop (clear)	Holiday shopping	English

Sky Digital 11.973V Tp14 Videoguard 27500 2/3 Sth45cm Nth60cm

Sony Entertainment TV	General entertainment	Hindi
Music Asia	Music	Hindi
Asia 1	General entertainment	Hindi
Minaj	General entertainment	Nigerian
Bangla	General entertainment	Bengali
Pakistani TV	General entertainment	Urdu

Sky Digital 11.992H Tp15 Videoguard 27500 2/3 Sth45cm Nth60cm

Open	Interactive shopping	English
Open	Promo	English

Sky Digital 12.012V Tp16 Videoguard 27500 2/3 Sth45cm Nth60cm

Open	Interactive shopping	English

Sky Digital 12.032H Tp17 Videoguard 27500 2/3 Sth45cm Nth60cm

Sky Digital 12.051V Tp18 Videoguard 27500 2/3 Sth45cm Nth60cm

Cartoon Network	Animation	English
TCM	Films	English
CNN	News (clear)	English
Travel	Holidays (clear)	English
Shop!	Home shopping (clear)	English
QVC	Home shopping (clear)	English

Sky Digital 12.070H Tp19 Videoguard 27500 2/3 Sth45cm Nth60cm

Sky Box Office	PPV channels	English
Cartoon Network + 1	Animation	English
Sky News	News (clear)	English
Sky Cinema	Films	English

Sky Digital 12.090V Tp20 Videoguard 27500 2/3 Sth45cm Nth60cm

Sky Box Office	PPV channels	English
The Disney Channel	Family entertainment	English
Sky Cinema 2	Films	English
Sky Digital Retail	Info	English

Sky Digital 12.109H Tp21 Videoguard 27500 2/3 Sth45cm Nth60cm

Sky Digital 12.246V Tp28 Videoguard 27500 2/3 Sth45cm Nth60cm

Sky Box Office	PPV channels	English
Sky Sports Extra	Interactive sports	English
Playboy/Adult Channel	Erotic fare	English
Fox Kids	Children's shows	English
Eurosport	Sports	English
Sky Business	Training	English

Sky Digital 12.266V Tp29 Videoguard 27500 2/3 Sth45cm Nth60cm

Sky Box Office	PPV channels	English
Fox Kids +1	Children's shows	English
Sky Moviemax 5	Films	English

Sky Digital 12.304H Tp31 Videoguard 27500 2/3 Sth45cm Nth60cm

Sky Box Office	PPV channels	English
Sky Sports Extra	Interactive sports	English

Sky Digital 12.364V Tp34 Videoguard 27500 2/3 Sth45cm Nth60cm

Test	Test card (clear)	–
Test	Test card (clear)	–
Test	Test card (clear)	–

Appendix C
Main broadcasting stations for terrestrial DTV

The UK has a total of six multiplexes, each offering a data capacity of 24.13 Mbit/s. Each multiplex contains between four and eight programmes. Five of the total number of programmes are digital versions of existing analogue programmes, leaving a capacity of about 30 new programmes. Two multiplexes are allocated for BBC and ITV. The remaining four (Mux A to Mux D) are for new broadcasters. The table lists the main transmitting stations for terrestrial DTV.

	D1 BBC		D2 ITV + 4		D3 Mux A		D4 Mux B		D5 Mux C		D6 Mux D	
	Ch	Pwr (kW)	Ch	Pwr (kW)	Ch	Pwr (kW)	Ch	Pwr (kW)	Ch	Pwr (kW)	Ch	Pwr (kW)
ENGLAND												
Beacon Hill	52	1.000	61	1.000	58	1.000	54	1.000	56	1.000	64	1.000
Belmont	30	5.000	48	10.000	68	10.000	66	10.000	60	4.000	57	4.000
Bilsdale	34	2.400	21	3.000	31	3.000	24	3.000	27	3.000	42	0.400
Bluebell Hill	59	3.000	24	2.000	27	2.000	45	3.000	42	3.000	39	3.000
Caldbeck	25	5.000	23	7.500	26	7.500	39	1.600	45	1.600	42	1.600
Caradon Hill	34	4.000	31	2.000	48	2.000	21	2.000	24	2.000	27	2.000
Chatton	40	3.000	50	3.000	43	3.000	46	1.000	47	1.000	51	1.000
Crystal Palace	25	6.500	22	6.500	32	6.500	28	6.500	34	1.000	29	1.000
Dover	61	1.000	68	1.000	55	1.000	58	1.000	57	1.000	60	0.500
Emley Moor	52	5.000	40	5.000	43	5.000	46	5.000	50	5.000	49	2.000
Hannington	50	10.000	43	5.000	40	5.000	46	5.000	29	1.300	48	0.850
Heathfield	34	1.600	29	1.600	48	2.500	47	1.000	54	1.000	51	1.000
Huntshaw Cross	54	2.000	58	2.000	61	2.000	64	2.000	53	2.000	57	2.000
Huntshaw Cross Fille									51	0.040	47	0.040
Mendip	59	3.000	55	3.000	62	3.000	65	3.000	52	0.250	48	0.250
Midhurst	56	10.000	65	10.000	62	2.500	59	2.500	64	1.000	60	1.000
Oxford	34	10.000	68	2.800	56	1.250	52	3.000	48	1.000	67	1.000
Plympton	52	0.100	67	0.100	66	0.100	60	0.100	63	0.100	56	0.100
Pontop Pike	48	10.000	55	10.000	59	10.000	62	10.000	65	10.000	53	2.000
Redruth	39	10.000	42	10.000	45	10.000	49	10.000	43	1.000	50	1.000
Ridge Hill	34	5.000	30	5.000	52	1.000	39	1.000	42	1.000	45	1.000
Rowridge	67	10.000	52	10.000	30	10.000	32	3.000	25	3.000	28	3.000
Sandy Heath	29	10.000	45	10.000	42	10.000	67	10.000	40	2.500	46	2.500
Stockland Hill	22	2.500	28	2.500	25	2.500	32	2.500	30	2.500	34	2.500
Sudbury	49	7.000	68	8.100	48	5.000	39	7.500	54	1.500	50	0.625
Sutton Coldfield	41	4.000	44	4.000	47	4.000	51	4.000	52	2.000	55	2.000

	Ch	kW	Ch	kW	Ch	kW	Ch	kW	Ch	kW	Ch	kW
Tacolneston	63	10.000	60	10.000	64	10.000	57	10.000	43	10.000	46	5.000
The Wrekin East	39	1.000	49	1.000	42	1.000	45	1.000	53	1.000	57	1.000
The Wrekin West	21	1.000	31	1.000	24	1.000	27	1.000	45	5.000	42	5.000
Waltham	49	5.000	23	10.000	26	10.000	33	10.000	60	2.000	63	2.000
Winter Hill	56	5.000	66	5.000	68	5.000	50	2.000				
CHANNEL ISLES												
Fremont Point	38	0.200	43	0.200	49	0.200	32	0.200	66	0.200	68	0.200
SCOTLAND												
Angus	68	2.000	66	2.000	59	2.000	62	2.000	56	2.000	65	2.000
Black Hill	41	10.000	47	10.000	44	10.000	51	10.000	55	10.000	65	10.000
Craigkelly	33	1.000	29	1.000	23	1.000	26	1.000	42	2.000	39	2.000
Darvel	22	2.000	25	2.000	32	2.000	28	2.000	30	2.000	34	2.000
Durris	30	10.000	34	10.000	52	10.000	51	5.000	41	5.000	44	5.000
Eitshal	34	0.800	30	0.800	22	0.800	25	0.800	28	0.800	32	0.800
Keelylang Hill	48	1.000	52	1.000	41	0.630	44	0.630	47	0.630	51	0.630
Knock More	34	1.000	30	1.000	53	1.000	57	1.000	60	1.000	56	1.000
Rosemarkie	47	10.000	51	10.000	41	10.000	44	10.000	46	4.000	50	4.000
Rumster Forest	28	1.000	22	1.000	25	1.000	32	1.000	62	2.000	59	2.000
Selkirk	53	3.000	57	3.000	60	3.000	63	3.000	66	0.500	56	0.500
NORTHERN IRELAND												
Brougher Mountain	30	0.500	34	0.500	23	0.500	26	0.500	29	0.500	33	0.500
Divis	29	8.900	33	8.900	23	8.900	26	8.900	48	1.800	34	0.800
Limavady	67	0.800	58	0.800	53	0.800	57	0.800	60	0.800	63	0.800
WALES												
Blaen Plwyf	28	2.000	22	2.000	25	2.000	32	2.000	29	1.000	33	1.000
Carmel	55	2.500	65	2.500	59	2.500	62	2.500	68	1.000	66	1.000
Llanddonna	67	1.000	54	1.000	58	1.000	61	1.000	64	1.000	46	0.500
Moel y Parc	54	0.500	58	0.500	61	0.500	64	0.500	30	0.250	34	0.250
Presely	47	0.500	51	0.500	39	1.000	42	1.000	45	1.000	49	1.000
Wenvoe	30	10.000	34	4.000	56	6.000	67	10.000				

Revision questions

1. With reference to main profile at single-level DTV broadcasting, state
   (a) number of pixels per line
   (b) total number of pixels per picture frame
   (c) the video sampling frequency
   (d) a typical FEC ratio

2. (a) Explain the need for data compression in DTV broadcasting.
   (b) State the two types of video data compression used in DTV broadcasting.
   (c) Explain what is meant by 'predicted picture'.

3. Refer to Fig. Q1.
   (a) Name the blocks X, Y and Z.
   (b) Describe the expected signals at points A, B, C and D.

4. Refer to Fig. Q1.
   (a) State the function of the modulator and give a brief explanation of its operation.
   (b) Describe the purpose of the high speed data port.

5. Refer to Fig. Q1. List the functions performed by the transport processor.

6. Figure Q2 shows a V/A processor chip.
   (a) State the function of each of the following pins indicating if the signal is an input or an output: pin 41, pin 1, pin 2, pin 77, pins 88–95, pin 100.
   (b) With regard to the AVDD bus, (i) state its bit width and (ii) explain its function.

7. Refer to Fig. Q2. For each of the following pins, state the function and the expected waveform: pin 96, pin 98, pin 133, pin 87, pin 57, pin 62.

8. Refer to Fig. Q2. State the effect of the following faults:
   (a) pin 75 stuck at one
   (b) pin 87 stuck at zero
   (c) pin 42 stuck at zero
   (d) pin 102 stuck at one

Fig. Q1

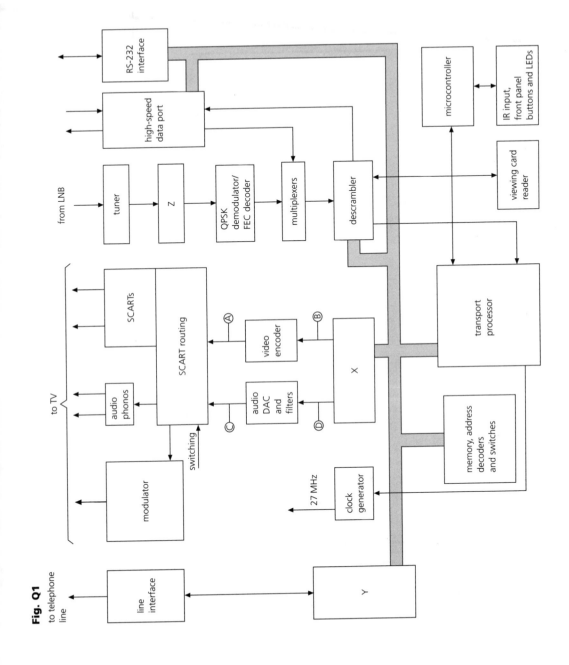

Fig. Q2

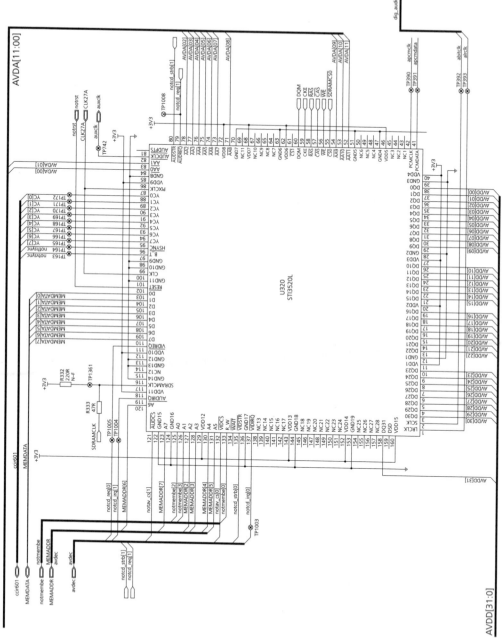

Fig. Q3

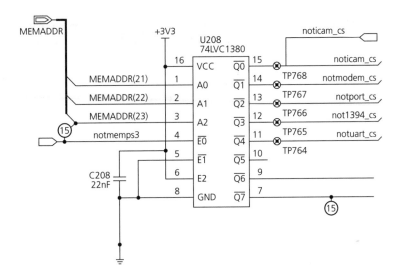

9. Refer to Fig. Q3.
   (a) State the function of U208.
   (b) Given that the logic levels of pins 1 to 3 are respectively 0, 0 and 1, state the expected logic levels of Q0–Q7.
   (c) State the effect of MEMADDR21 stuck at zero.

10. (a) State the type of modulation used in DTV-T (terrestrial) and DTV-S (satellite).
    (b) Explain the reasons for using different types of modulation in DTV broadcasting.

11. In audio compression, what is meant by masking? State a typical sampling rate.

12. With reference to a packetized elementary stream (PES), state (a) its function, (b) some different types and (c) the purpose and size of the header.

13. Give a brief explanation of the following terms: FEC, APT, transport stream, PCR, PID.

14. In a set-top box, explain the purpose of
    (a) the transport demultiplexer
    (b) the PAL encoder
    (c) the descrambler
    (d) the SCART router

Answers to selected questions

1. (a) 720
   (b) $720 \times 576 = 414\,720$
   (c) 27 MHz
   (d) 2/3 or 3/4

3. (a) X is A/V decoder
       Y is modem
       Z is ADC
   (b) waveform at A is CVBS (composite video)
       waveform at B is digitized and multiplexed luminance/chrominance
       waveform at C is audio left and right
       waveform at D is PCM audio

6. (a) pin 41 is audio PCM
       pin 1 is L/R select
       pin 2 is audio serial clock
       pin 77 is video memory address line
       pins 88–95 are the luminance/chrominance multiplexed 8-bit bus
   (b) The AVDD bus is the video memory address bus; it is 32 bits wide

7. pin 96 is horizontal sync pulse
   pin 98 is 0 V line
   pin 133 is read/write line; digital activity
   pin 87 is 27 MHz clock pulse
   pin 57 is column address select for video memory; digital activity
   pin 52 is 3.3 V DC

8. (a) picture break-up leading to total failure
   (b) decoder failure; no picture
   (c) no sound
   (d) no effect; reset must be high all the time

9. (a) address decoder
   (b) Q0–Q2 low, Q3 high, Q4–Q7 low
   (c) Some processing chips will never be selected, leading to complete video
       and audio failure

Glossary

Access time	A measure of the speed of a storage device such as a memory chip. Defined as the time interval between the instant when an address appears on the address bus and data appearing on the data bus
Access unit (AU)	Coded representation of a video frame or an audio piece
Active high	Applies to hardware control signals which are active, i.e. perform their task, when their logic state is high (or logic 1)
Active low	applies to hardware control signals which are active, i.e. perform their task, when their logic state is low (or logic 0). Hardware control signals, such as reset, enable and chip select, are normally active low
Adaptation field (AF)	Data field used to adapt the relatively long PES packet to the much shorter 188-byte transport stream packet length
Adaptive quantizing	Quantizing in which some parameters are varied in accordance with the importance of the data being transmitted
ADC	Analogue-to-digital converter
ADSL	Asynchronous digital subscriber line
AFC	Automatic frequency control used to lock onto and maintain the selected channel frequency
AGC	Automatic gain control used to vary the gain of the tuner or other amplifiers in order to keep the output constant
Aliasing	Distortion caused when an analogue signal is sampled at or below the Nyquist rate of $2 \times$ the highest analogue frequency
Alignment	Fine adjustment of an antenna for optimum signal strength
ALU	Arithmetic and logic unit. The part of the CPU which carries out the arithmetic and logic operations
Anchor picture	Reference frame used when obtaining predicted frames
ANSI	American National Standards Institute
Aspect ratio	The ratio between the width and the height of a TV screen
ATM	Asynchronous transfer mode. Protocol for transporting data in a digital network based on the transfer of units of information known as cells
Azimuth (AZ)	The angle between an antenna beam and the north–south line
Baseband	Original frequency bandwidth of an analogue or digital signal
Baseband transmission	Transmission which uses the entire spectrum of the medium for one channel
Baud	A measure of the speed of a data stream given in symbols per second

B frame	Bidirectional frame. A predicted frame constructed by using past and future predicted frames
Bit error rate (BER)	A measurement of the accuracy of a received bitstream stated in terms of the ratio of error bits to the total number of bits
Bit rate	A measure of the speed of a data stream given in bits per second
Block	An 8×8 matrix of pixels or DCT coefficients
Block coding	A coding technique where a block of k data items is encoded into a longer code word of n digits by adding $n - k$ redundancy bits
Bouquet	A group of transport streams from different networks
Buffer memory	A storage area which provides an uninterrupted flow of data delivered at a constant rate
Burst errors	Adjacent multiple error bits
Byte	A group of 8 bits
CAM	Conditional access module
CAT	Conditional access table
Chipset	Several chips designed to work together to perform a defined operation
Chrominance	Colour components of a video signal
CNR	Carrier-to-noise ratio. It measures the effect of noise on the received signal
Codec	Coder/decoder
Code rate	The ratio $k{:}n$ where k is the number of digits of a code and $n - k$ is the number of redundant bits added to the code for error correction capabilities
Code vector	Another name for a code word
Code word	A valid code from among all available codes, also known as a code vector, or vector for short
COFDM	Coded orthogonal frequency division multiplexing. To reduce the effect of frequency-dependent noise in terrestrial DTV broadcasting, OFDM is coded to improve the error correction capabilities of the system
Companding	Reduction of noise by compression at the transmitter and subsequent expansion at the receiver
Composite video	Analogue video signal which includes the video information together with blanking and sync pulses, also known as CVBS
Conditional access (CA)	System to control subscriber access to programmes
Constellation map	A map showing all possible phases and amplitudes of the carrier for PSK or QAM modulation
Convolutional coding	A coding technique where the code word is determined by the previous code word as well as the block of bits presented for encoding. This provides a more robust system for error correction than the simple block coding technique
CPU	Central processing unit, normally known as the microprocessor
CRC	Cyclic redundancy check. A technique used to detect errors in data transmission
CS	Chip select. A hardware chip control signal which enables the chip
CSI	Channel state information. Information used at the receiver which, when combined with FEC, ensures that frequency-dependent noise is corrected
CVBS	Composite video, blanking and sync

DAB	Digital audio broadcasting
DAC	Digital-to-analogue converter
dB	Decibel, a unit for measuring relative power
dBm	Decibel-milliwatt, a unit for measuring power relative to 1 mW
DBS	Direct broadcast satellite
DCT	Discrete cosine transform. The process of transforming the pixel values of a block into coefficients representing the spatial frequency components of the image represented by the block
Demodulation	The recovery of the signal information from the modulated carrier
Demultiplexing	The separation of multiplexed signals. The reverse of multiplexing
Descrambling	A system for returning scrambled signals back to their original state
Differential coding	Coding the difference between values instead of their absolute values
Downconversion	The process of changing a frequency from a high band to a lower band
Downlink	The signal path from the satellite to a receiving dish
DPSK	Differential phase shift keying. A PSK technique which encodes the difference between successive phases
DQPSK	Differential quadrature phase shift keying
DRAM	Dynamic RAM. A type of read/write memory which requires regular refreshing of its contents
DSL	Digital subscriber line which provides fast access to telephone subscribers. There are several DSL protocols, including ADSL, ISDN and ATM
DSP	Digital signal processor
DTH	Direct to home, mainly satellite communication
DTS	Decoding time stamp. Part of the PES header which indicates the moment when an access unit (AU) should be decoded
DTTV	Digital terrestrial television
DTV	Digital television
DVB	Digital video broadcasting
DVB-C	Digital video broadcasting for cable applications
DVB-S	Digital video broadcasting for satellite applications
DVB-T	Digital video broadcasting for terrestrial applications
DVD	Digital versatile disk. Also known as digital videodisc
EEPROM	Electrically erasable PROM. EEPROM can be programmed and erased while in circuit
Elementary stream (ES)	Video, audio or service compressed data stream
Elevation	The angle between the antenna beam and the horizontal plane
EN	Enable. A hardware chip control signal similar to chip select (CS)
Encryption	A method of encoding information so that access by subscribers may be controlled
Energy dispersal	A technique to obtain even distribution of energy in digital transmission
EOB	End of block. A code used in DCT scanning to indicate that the remaining DCT coefficients of a block are all zero
EPG	Electronic programme guide
EPROM	Erasable PROM
ERP	Effective radiated power

FEC	Forward error correction. The addition of redundant bits to a code word so that errors introduced by the transmission medium may be detected and corrected at the receiving end
FFT	Fast Fourier transform
Field	In an interlaced video signal, the complete picture frame is divided into two fields, a top field containing the odd scan-lines and a bottom field containing the even scan-lines
Flash	A programmable memory store which retains its data when power is switched off
Fourier transform	A process for analysing a signal into its frequency components
Frame	A complete scanned TV picture
Frequency multiplexing	The allocation of part of the available bandwidth to different channels or programmes
GOP	Group of pictures, normally 12, having the same reference picture frame (I frame) and containing several predicted frames
GPIO	General-purpose input/output
Gray code	A binary counting sequence that ensures only one binary bit changes state when the count is incremented or decremented
Guard interval	Time interval during which the DTV terrestrial receiver is not responsive to the received signal. It is used to avoid the effect of delay signals due to reflection
HD	High definition
HDTV	High definition television employing more than 1000 scan-lines
Head end	The central distribution point in any broadcasting network which receives and generates signals
Hex	Hexadecimal. A numbering system with a base of 16
I/O	Input/output
I^2C bus	Inter IC bus. A two-line serial control bus
IFFT	Inverse fast Fourier transform
I frame	A reference frame for a group of pictures
IM bus	Intermetall bus. A three-line serial control bus
Intercoding	Data compression produced by comparing successive frames
Interlacing	A video scanning technique which produces two fields for each complete picture frame: an odd (top) field with odd scan-lines and an even (bottom) field with even scan-lines
Interleaving	A technique used to break up bursts of errors to improve error correction
Intracoding	Data compression within one frame
IRD	Integrated receiver decoder. The set-top box which receives and decodes digital television signals
IRQ	Interrupt request. A hardware interrupt used in microprocessor-based systems to request a service from the CPU
ISDN	Integrated services digital network. Fast data stream (64 or 128 kbit/s) used over standard telephone lines
LNB	Low noise block. A downcoverter used to convert satellite signals received by the dish into an intermediate frequency known as the first IF
Loop-through	A facility provided by the UHF modulator of a set-top box to allow external UHF signals, such as analogue broadcasts, to be sent out to the same UHF output socket

LPF	Lowpass filter
LSB	Least significant bit. The rightmost bit of a binary number
Luminance	Black and white content of a picture
Macroblock	Picture space of 16×16 pixels
Masking	The exclusion of sound perception by the human ear due to the presence of other sounds
Master clock	A clock that is used to control all other clocks
Modem	Modulator/demodulator used as interface between a device and the telephone system
Motion compensation	The technique of estimating the motion vector of a block of pixels during video encoding
Motion vector	A vector that represents the direction and speed of the estimated motion of a block of pixels
MPEG	Motion Picture Expert Group
MSB	Most significant bit. The leftmost bit in a binary number
Multiplexing	The process of combining a number of independent signals to share a single transmission medium
MUSICAM	Masking universal sub-band integrated coding and multiplexing. A technique employed in MPEG audio coding
MUX	Multiplexer
NICAM	Near instantaneous companded audio multiplexing. A high quality digital stereophonic sound coding system used in analogue TV broadcasting
NIT	Network information table
NTSC	National Television System Committee. A television system used in the USA
Null packets	Packets that carry no data but are necessary to maintain a constant bit rate
OE	Output enable. A hardware chip control signal. It has the same effect as the RD control signal.
OFDM	Orthogonal frequency division multiplexing. A modulation technique used in terrestrial digital TV broadcasting. It employs a large number of equally spaced orthogonal carriers: 2048 (2K mode) or 8192 (8K mode)
Orthogonal	At right angles to each other.
OSD	Onscreen display. The displaying of various information on a TV screen such as programme number, date and other messages
Padding	Non-significant bits that are added to ensure a constant bit rate
PAL	Phase alternate line. A television system used in the UK
PAT	Programme allocation table. A table which lists the PID of each available programme
Payload	Contents of a packet of data other than the header
PCM	Pulse code modulation. A modulation technique which samples the analogue signal then represents each sample by a binary code
PCR	Programme clock reference. A sample of the system clock at the transmitter is sent along the data stream in the form of a count; it is used for time synchronization at the receiving end
PES	Packetized elementary stream
P frame	Predicted frame

PID	Packet identifier. A 13-bit code included in the header of the transport stream packet to identify the programme that the particular packet belongs to
Pixel	Picture element. The smallest element of a picture
PLL	Phase-locked loop. Used to ensure the synchronization of two clocks
PMT	Programme map table. It indicates the PID of the packetized elementary stream (PES) where the PAT is to be found
PRBS	Pseudo-random binary sequence ˙
Pre-emphasis	A technique which increases the amplitude of high frequency signals before modulation to improve their SNR. The process is reversed at the receiving end (de-emphasis)
Progressive scanning	A scanning process which produces a single picture frame containing all the scan-lines, odd and even
PROM	Programmable ROM
PSI	Programme-specific information which keeps track of the different programmes contained within the transport stream
PSK	Phase shift keying. A technique used for modulating digital signals by using the phase of the carrier to represent one or more bits
PSTN	Public switched telephone network. The public telephone system
PTS	Presentation time stamp. It indicates the time an access unit must be presented to the viewer
Puncturing	A technique used to reduce redundancy and hence the bit rate, by removing a part of the bitstream at the expense of robustness to errors
PWM	Pulse width modulation. A modulation technique whereby the width of the pulse changes in accordance with the signal
QAM	Quadrature amplitude modulation. A type of PSK modulation in which the carrier amplitude is also changed to provide a higher baud rate
QEF	Quasi-error-free. A system is described as QEF if the bit error rate (BER) is less than one in 10^{11}
QPSK	Quadrature phase shift keying where each phase is used to represent a group of two bits
Quantizing	The process of determining the level of a sample within a given number of discrete levels
Quantizing error	An error in a digital system caused by the inherent ambiguity in the least significant bit
RAM	Random access memory. A read/write memory store which loses its data if power is switched off
RD	Read. A hardware chip control signal which instructs the chip to place data on its data bus
Redundancy	The inclusion of extra bits in a code to improve error detection and correction at the receiving end
Reed–Solomon coding	A coding technique in which DVB adds 16 parity bytes to the 188-byte transport stream packet. It allows corrections of up to 8 bytes of errors in any one packet
REST	*See* RST
RLC	Run-length coding. A coding method which encodes a series of identical bits as a group instead of encoding them individually

RS-232	A bidirectional serial link standard used for intercommunication between various devices
RST	Reset. A hardware chip control signal which resets a programmable chip such as a CPU or a video/audio decoder
Sampling	The process of taking samples of an analogue signal, usually at regular intervals
Sampling rate	The number of samples taken per second
Scalable coding	A coding technique which provides two layers: a lower layer with certain restrained picture resolution and an upper layer with high picture resolution
SCART	A 21-pin connector used for interconnection between TV receivers, VCRs, IRDs and other systems
SCL	Serial clock for the I^2C serial control bus
Scrambling	A method of coding aimed at restricting access by subscribers
SDA	Serial data for the I^2C serial control bus
SECAM	A television system used in France
Set-top box (STB)	A popular name for the integrated receiver decoder (IRD)
SFN	Single-frequency network. The use of a single carrier frequency for broadcasting to all regions
SNR	Signal-to-noise ratio
Sparklies	Popular name for noise which appears in the form of black and white flashes on the screen. Normally associated with analogue satellite reception where the CNR is low
Spatial compression	Intraframe data reduction which removes unnecessary repetition of video information within a single picture frame
SRAM	Static RAM. A fast type of RAM chip that does not require refreshing
SSB	Single sideband
Statistical multiplexing	Multiplexing which allocates different time slots for different signals according to need
Subcarrier	A carrier that falls within the spectrum of another carrier. In analogue television, colour information is used to modulate a subcarrier of 4.41 MHz which falls within the 5 MHz bandwidth of the monochrome video signal
Symbol	A group of bits represented by a single change in carrier phase, carrier amplitude or both
Symbol rate	The number of carrier transitions (e.g. phase changes) per second Each such transition may represent a group of two, four or more bits. Also known as the baud rate, the symbol rate is not the same as the bit rate; bit rate specifies the number of bits per second
System-on-a-chip (SOC)	A chip that combines the core of a microprocessor with embedded memory, I/O ports, UART and external bus interface. SOC devices carry out general processing tasks as well as dedicated processing operations such as transport demultiplexing
TDM	Time division multiplexing. A process where several channels are interleaved in time so that they may share a single transmission medium
Temporal compression	Interframe data reduction which removes similarities between successive frames

TPS	Transmission parameter signalling. Bits are scattered within the DVB-T broadcast to provide transmission parameters such as mode, guard period, modulation type
Transponder	The active part of a satellite which, following amplification and frequency change, rebroadcasts the received information on the uplink from the transmitting station on Earth
Transport stream (TS)	Data stream containing compressed data in the form of multiplexed packetized elementary streams of several programmes within a single channel suitable for modulation and transmission
UART	Universal asynchronous receiver transmitter. An interface which provides serial communication between devices such as a set-top box and a modem
UHF	Ultra high frequency. Frequency band from 330 MHz to 3 GHz. A part of the UHF band (470–790 MHz) is allocated for terrestrial TV broadcasting
Uplink	The transmission path from the earth station to a satellite
VCO	Voltage-controlled oscillator
Viterbi	A decoding technique which is very effective for convolutionally coded data streams
VOD	Video on demand. System in which video programmes are transmitted to a subscriber when requested
Volatile	A memory store that loses its data when DC power to it is removed
WR	Write. A hardware chip control signal that instructs data to be written into the chip
Zigzag scanning	Sequence of scanning DCT coefficients so that those most likely to have zero value appear at the end of the scan

References

BBC 1997 Digital terrestrial television. *BBC Research and Development Annual Review 1997*

Beniot H. 1999 *Satellite techniques of analogue and digital television* Edward Arnold, London

Bower A.J. 1998 Digital radio – the Eureka 147 DAB system. *Electronic Engineering,* April 1998

Breed J. 1997 *The satellite book* SWIFT, London

Cutts D.J. 1996 DVD conditional access. In *Proceedings of the International Broadcast Convention*, 12–16 Sept 1996

Ely S.R. 1995 MPEG video: a simple introduction. *EBU Technical Review* **Winter** 1995

Hurley T.R. 1996 Evolution of the digital set-top box. In *Proceedings of the International Broadcast Convention*, 12–16 Sept 1996

Kraal C.J. 1996 Development of interactive services in digital TV. In *Proceedings of the International Broadcast Convention*, 12–16 Sept 1996

Mitchell J.D. and Sadot P. 1996 Development of a digital terrestrial front end. In *Proceedings of the International Broadcast Convention*, 12–16 Sept 1996

Moller G. 1995 Digital terrestrial television: the 8K system. *EBU Technical Review* **Winter** 1995

Nokes C.R., Pullen I.R. and Salter J.E. 1997 Evaluation of a DVB-T compliant digital terrestrial television system. In *Proceedings of the International Broadcast Convention*, Amsterdam, 12–16 Sept 1997, pp. 331–6

Reimers U. 1997 The COFDM-based system for terrestrial television. *Electronics and Communication Engineering Journal*, Feb 1997

Stott J.H. 1997 Exploring some of the magic of COFDM. In *Proceedings of the 20th International Television Symposium*, Moutreux, Switzerland, 13–17 June

Tudor N.P. 1995 MPEG-2 video compression. *Electronics and Communication Engineering Journal*, Dec 1995

Van de Laar F., Philips N. and Olde Dubbelink R. 1993 General-purpose and application-specific design of a DAB channel decoder. *EBU Technical Review* **Winter** 1993

Walters G.T. 1996 Television in the digital era. *EBU Technical Review* **Autumn** 1996

Watkinson J. 1999 *MPEG-2* Focal Press, London

Index